JEAN-FRANÇOIS MALLET

SIMPLE HEALTHY

THE EASIEST LIGHT COOKBOOK IN THE WORLD

**Light French-inspired recipes to read at
a glance and make in a flash**

BLACK DOG
& LEVENTHAL
PUBLISHERS
NEW YORK

This is not a diet cookbook but rather a collection of light (or lighter) recipes that are healthy, tasty, and varied. It comes in response to a question I am regularly asked by my friends, both women and men: how do you live on ordinary everyday food without putting on weight and only eating three lettuce leaves, a yogurt, and an apple?

It is possible to enjoy your food while keeping an eye on your figure and your health, create new dishes that provide five fruits and vegetables a day, and only use a few ingredients you have in your refrigerator or pantry, or that are easy to find in the local grocery store.

In this, my second book, I want to share everyday recipes with you that are quick and easy and will satisfy all tastes. Combining simple flavors and ingredients makes it perfectly possible to prepare light, delicious dishes, and even create the occasional sensation, without spending hours in the kitchen.

The recipes, which use three to five ingredients, are clearly explained and extremely simple to make. You will learn to steam everything, even very rare red meat. You will make delicious, super-light, classic sauces—even mayonnaise—which will become the core of your meal when accompanied by grilled meat, vegetables, or salad. You will discover that a stock based on green tea, fish cooked in parchment paper or aluminum foil, or a joint of meat cooked in water can become everyday dishes.

Have a great time in your kitchen and enjoy eating food that will keep you slim and fit.

CONTENTS

HOW TO USE THIS BOOK

In this book I assume that you have at home:

- Running water
- A stovetop and oven
- A refrigerator
- A frying pan
- A cast iron casserole
- A knife (very sharp)
- Salt and pepper
- Oil; extra-virgin olive oil is best, but also hazelnut, sesame, and walnut oils

(If this is not the case, maybe now is the time to invest!)

The essential investment

- **A steamer:** ideally one with a timer, which will save you a considerable amount of time and guarantee the success of some of the reci pes in this book. (See more on page 7.)

What are the must-have ingredients?

- **Fresh rather than canned:** you will find almost no canned goods in this book, apart from indispensables like coconut milk and tomato purée.
- **Frozen:** even though you are using mainly fresh products, it is sometimes easier to buy frozen products, such as peas, seafood, and some fillets of fish.
- **Herbs:** there is nothing to equal fresh herbs. If you run out, you can always use the frozen or dried versions (but they are not as good).
- **Oils:** olive oil (always use extra-virgin [that is the best]), and have hazelnut, sesame, and walnut oils.
- **Fruit and vegetables:** use fruit and vegetables that are in season and—though this is not obligatory—preferably organic, especially lemons, because the peel is used often.
- **Soy sauce:** preferably use the Japanese Kikkoman® type, the one with the green top, which is less salty.

Which techniques should you use?

- **Cooking in a double boiler or bain-marie:** this technique allows you to melt or cook a food without burning it. Place the bowl or pan containing the food inside or on top of another, larger pan of boiling water.
- **Marinating:** soaking an ingredient in an aromatic mixture to flavor or tenderize it.
- **Beating egg whites until stiff:** add a pinch of salt to the egg whites and use an electric mixer, gradually increasing the speed. Always beat the whites in the same direction to prevent them from going grainy.
- **Peeling an orange:** remove the peel and the white pith with a knife. Cut off both ends of the orange and gradually remove the peel by sliding the knife blade between the peel and the fruit, working from top to bottom.

- **Reducing:** reducing the quantity of a *jus* or stock by evaporation over heat (without the lid), while keeping it on the boil. This process concentrates the flavors and gives a smoother consistency.
- **Zesting a lemon:** there are three ways to zest a lemon. If you are a beginner and you want a very fine zest, use a cheese grater on the lemon's peel, going over each area just once, without touching the white pith. If you are a professional and you want zest that looks like vermicelli, use a zester. If you are resourceful and you want something like shavings, use a paring knife.

Steaming

Steaming is dull and insipid, so they say . . .

Dismiss this received wisdom from your mind: steaming is light, because no fat is used. It is just cooking in the oven and in water at the same time, while preserving the food's vitamins. This method of cooking is ideal for vegetables, fish, poultry, and tender white meat. On the other hand, it is rarely recommended for red meat. However, if you follow the instructions in this book to the letter, you will be able to produce meat that is rare and juicy.

What equipment should you choose?

- **Steamer:** this is the ideal appliance for cooking without needing to keep an eye on it all the time. Consisting of two or three baskets piled one on top of the other, it enables you to cook the starter and the main course at the same time.
- **Electric mixer:** its beaters are perfect for mixing sauces, beating egg whites stiff, or whipping cream. It can be replaced with a hand whisk and elbow grease!
- **Hand blender:** also known as a stick or immersion blender, this is used to mix liquids (soups, smoothies, milkshakes, etc.). It is very handy, inexpensive, space-saving, and also means less washing up, because it is used directly in whatever you are mixing with no need to transfer it to a different bowl.
- **Blender:** this is more expensive than a hand blender and takes up more space but produces a smoother, creamier result—though more washing up as well, because the liquid to be mixed has to be transferred to the blender bowl.
- **Multifunctional food processor:** as its name suggests, this is a multipurpose machine. It has various tools for such functions as chopping, whisking, slicing, mincing, and emulsifying.

What oven settings?

200°F/90°C: 3	300°F/150°C: 5	400°F/210°C: 7	500°F/270°C: 9
250°F/120°C: 4	350°F/180°C: 6	450°F/240°C: 8	575°F/300°C: 10

That is everything.
All you have to do now is follow the recipe!

BREADSTICKS WITH SESAME SEEDS

364 kcal/person

—

Vegetarian

—

Gluten free

Buckwheat flour
1⅔ cups (200 g)

Almond flour
¾ cup plus
1 tablespoon (80 g)

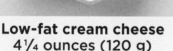

Low-fat cream cheese
4¼ ounces (120 g)

Sesame seeds
2 tablespoons (16 g)

Preparation: 15 minutes
Cooking: 10 minutes

• Preheat the oven to 350°F/180°C. Mix the **buckwheat flour**, **almond flour**, and **cream cheese** into a smooth dough.

• Divide the dough into small balls, shape into sticks, and sprinkle with **sesame seeds**.

• Arrange the sticks in an ovenproof dish lined with parchment paper and bake for 10 minutes. Serve warm, with mashed avocados, if desired.

PARSNIP HUMMUS WITH CILANTRO

68 kcal/person

—

Vegetarian

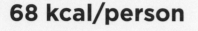

Parsnips
x 2

Cilantro
1 bunch

Curry powder
2 tablespoons (13 g)

Plain Greek yogurt
2 tablespoons (30 g)

Olive oil
1 tablespoon (15 mL)

 **Salt, pepper**

🕐
Preparation: 15 minutes
Cooking: 25 minutes

• Peel the **parsnips** and steam for 25 minutes. Chop the **cilantro**.

• Mash with a potato masher, then add the chopped **cilantro**, **curry powder**, **yogurt**, and **olive oil**. Season with salt and pepper and mix. Serve cold with crudités.

PEAR SPRING ROLLS

107 kcal/person

—

Gluten free

—

Lactose free

Pears
x 2

Cilantro
1 bunch

Arugula
3½ ounces (100 g)

Rice paper wrappers
x 8 (8½ inches, or 21 cm)

Bresaola
4 slices

Preparation: 10 minutes

• Peel the **pears** and cut into eighths. Chop the **cilantro** and **arugula**.
• Shortly before serving, soak the **rice paper wrappers** in a bowl of water and arrange on the work surface, smooth-side down.
• Spread the bresaola, pears, and herbs on the **rice paper wrappers**, then roll up tightly. Serve whole or cut into bite-size pieces.

SHRIMP SPRING ROLLS

70 kcal/person
—
Gluten free
—
Lactose free

Cooked shrimp
x 24

Kiwi
x 2

Cilantro
1 bunch

Mint
18 leaves

Rice paper wrappers
x 8 (8½ inches, or 21 cm)

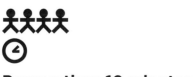

Preparation: 10 minutes

• Peel the **shrimp**. Cut the **kiwi** into eighths. Chop the **cilantro** and **mint**.

• Shortly before serving, soak the **rice paper wrappers** in a bowl of water and arrange on the work surface, smooth-side down.

• Spread the filling ingredients on the **rice paper wrappers**, then roll up tightly. Serve whole or cut into bite-size pieces.

SALMON SPRING ROLLS

112 kcal/person

—

Gluten free

—

Lactose free

Green apples
x 2

Lettuce
4 leaves

Rice paper wrappers
x 8 (8½ inches, or 21 cm)

Smoked salmon
8 thin slices

Basil
16 leaves

Preparation: 10 minutes

• Peel the **apples** and cut into thin slices. Separate the **lettuce leaves**.

• Shortly before serving, soak the **rice paper wrappers** in a bowl of water and arrange on the work surface, smooth-side down. Spread the **salmon**, **lettuce**, **apples**, and **basil** on the **rice paper wrappers**, then roll up tightly. Serve whole or cut into bite-size pieces.

CHICKEN AND ZUCCHINI SKEWERS

224 kcal/person

—

Gluten free

—

Lactose free

Chicken breasts
x 2

Zucchini
x 1

Olive oil
2 tablespoons (30 mL)

Organic lemons
x 2

Dried thyme leaves
1 tablespoon (3 g)

Salt, pepper

Preparation: 20 minutes
Marinating: 30 minutes
Cooking: 20 minutes

• Preheat the oven to 350°F/180°C. Cut the **chicken** in strips and slice the **zucchini** in strips lengthwise with a paring knife. Thread the strips onto wooden skewers and marinate for 30 minutes in the **olive oil**, grated **lemon** zest, **lemon** juice, and **thyme**. Season with salt and pepper. Bake for 20 minutes. Serve hot or cold.

TAHITIAN-STYLE RAW FISH

422 kcal/person

—

Gluten free

—

Lactose free

Swordfish
1 pound, 5 ounces (600 g)

Limes
x 4

Cilantro
1 bunch

Carrot
x 1 large

Coconut milk
1²/₃ cups (400 ml)

 **Salt**, pepper

Preparation: 15 minutes
Marinating: 5 minutes

• Cut the **fish** into cubes and squeeze the **limes**. Chop the **cilantro** leaves and some of the stems, then peel the **carrot** and grate with a hand grater.
• Mix all the ingredients together in a salad bowl. Season with salt and pepper, leave to marinate for 5 minutes in the refrigerator, and then serve.

EGGPLANT ROULADES

129 kcal/person

—

Gluten free

Eggplant
x 1 large or 2 small

Fresh goat cheese
4¼ ounces (120 g)

Dried thyme leaves
1 tablespoon (3 g)

Cooked ham
4 slices without rind

 **1 drizzle olive oil**

Preparation: 25 minutes
Cooking: 20 minutes

- Cut the **eggplant** into 12 slices lengthwise and cook for 20 minutes in a steamer.
- Mix the **goat cheese** with the **thyme**. Cut the **ham** slices into thirds.
- Place a slice of **ham** on each slice of **eggplant**. Spread with the **cheese** mixture and roll up.
- Serve with a drizzle of olive oil.

CLAMS WITH AVOCADO

187 kcal/person

—

Gluten free

—

Lactose free

Clams
x 30 (cleaned)

Avocado
x 1

Limes
x 3

Olive oil
1 tablespoon (15 mL)

Dill
1 bunch

Preparation: 20 minutes
Cooking: 10 minutes

• Cook the **clams** in 7 fluid ounces (200 mL) water over high heat until they open. Drain and strain the liquid.

• Mix **lime** juice with diced **avocado**, **olive oil**, chopped **dill**, and 5 ounces (150 mL) cooking liquid.

• Remove the upper half of the shell, arrange the **clams** on plates, and garnish with the **avocado** mixture. Serve warm or cold.

PORK AND SHRIMP NIBBLES

128 kcal/person

—

Steam

—

Gluten free

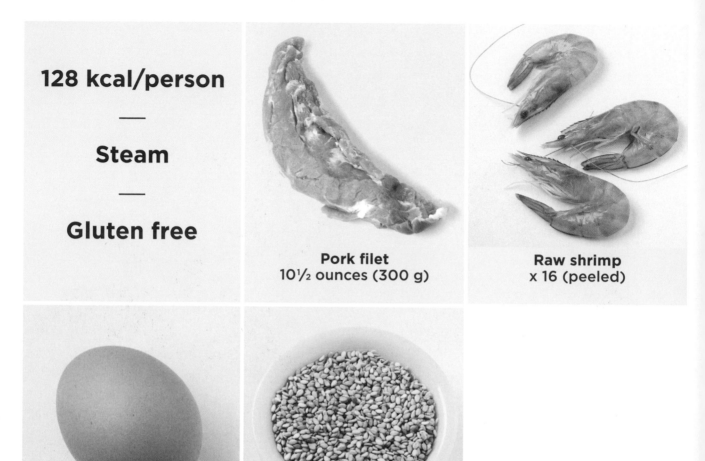

Pork filet
10½ ounces (300 g)

Raw shrimp
x 16 (peeled)

Egg
x 1

Sesame seeds
1 tablespoon (8 g)

 Salt, pepper

1 drizzle sesame oil

Preparation: 20 minutes
Cooking: 10 minutes

• In a blender, mix together the **pork**, half the **shrimp**, and the **egg**.
• Chop the remaining **shrimp** and add to the mixture. Season and place bite-size mounds of the mixture on squares of baking paper.
• Cook for 10 minutes in a steamer. Sprinkle with **sesame seeds** and serve warm or cold with a drizzle of sesame oil.

BASS WITH GRAPEFRUIT

194 kcal/person

—

Gluten free

—

Lactose free

Pink grapefruit
x 1

Olive oil
3 tablespoons (45 mL)

Bass fillets
1 pound (455 g), skinless

Cilantro
½ bunch

 **Salt, pepper**

👨‍👩‍👧‍👦

🕐
Preparation: 15 minutes

• Squeeze the **grapefruit**, strain the juice, and mix with the **olive oil**.
• Cut the **bass** into thin slices. Chop the **cilantro**.
• Arrange the fish slices on plates. Add the **grapefruit** juice mixture and **cilantro**. Season with salt and pepper and serve.

TERRINE OF CHICKEN WITH PRESERVED LEMONS

262 kcal/person

—

Gluten free

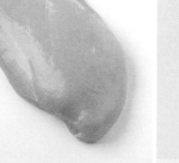
**Chicken breasts
x 2**

**Eggs
x 2**

**Low-fat cream cheese
4¼ ounces (120 g)**

**Preserved lemons
x 2**

**Fresh baby spinach
5 ounces (150 g)**

Salt, pepper

1 drizzle olive oil for the mold

**Preparation: 25 minutes
Cooking: 40 minutes**

• Preheat the oven to 350°F/180°C. In a food processor, blend the **chicken** with the **eggs**, **cream cheese**, salt, and pepper. Dice the **lemons** and add to the mixture with the **spinach**.

• Transfer to a lightly oiled nonstick mold and bake for 40 minutes.

• Turn out the hot terrine, chill, and serve cold with lettuce.

ASPARAGUS WITH MOUSSELINE SAUCE

91 kcal/person

—

Vegetarian

—

Gluten free

Egg
x 1

Low-fat cream cheese
4¼ ounces (120 g)

Mustard
1 teaspoon

Chives
1 bunch

Green asparagus
2 bunches

Salt, pepper

Preparation: 15 minutes
Cooking: 5 minutes

• Separate the **egg**. Mix the yolk with the **cream cheese**, **mustard**, and chopped **chives**. Season with salt and pepper.
• Whisk the egg white with a whisk until stiff and fold it gently into the **mustard** mixture. Trim the **asparagus** but do not peel. Steam for 5 minutes. Serve warm with the cold sauce.

HOT LIVER WITH CHANTERELLES

216 kcal/person

—

Gluten free

Chanterelles
9 ounces (250 g)

Chicken livers
9 ounces (250 g)

Eggs
x 3

Low-fat cream cheese
4¼ ounces (120 g)

Thyme
4 sprigs

 Salt, **pepper**

Preparation: 20 minutes
Cooking: 25 minutes

• Preheat the oven to 350°F/180°C. Clean the **chanterelles** and cut into pieces.

• In a blender, mix the **chicken livers** with the **eggs**, **cream cheese**, salt, and pepper. Fold in the **chanterelles** and transfer to 4 ramekins. Top each ramekin with a sprig of **thyme** and bake in a bain-marie for 25 minutes. Eat warm.

WARM CARROTS WITH SAFFRON SAUCE

191 kcal/person

—

Vegetarian

Carrots with tops
x 16 (medium)

Eggs
x 2

Low-fat cream cheese
4¼ ounces (120 g)

Saffron threads
1 heaping teaspoon (1 g)

 **Salt**, **pepper**

Preparation: 15 minutes
Cooking: 30 minutes

• Peel the **carrots** and cook for 30 minutes in a steamer.

• Separate the **eggs**. Mix the yolks with the **cream cheese** and **saffron**. Season with salt and pepper.

• Before serving, beat egg whites until stiff, then fold into the **saffron** mixture. Serve **carrots** warm with the cold sauce and season with sea salt.

EGGS WITH MAYONNAISE

212 kcal/person

—

Vegetarian

—

Gluten free

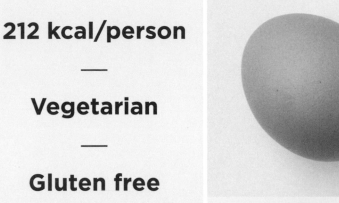
Eggs
x 6 (4 whole + 2 yolks)

Strong mustard
2 tablespoons (30 g)

Low-fat cream cheese
8½ ounces (240 g)

Lettuce head
x 1 (small)

 **Salt, pepper**

Preparation: 5 minutes
Cooking: 10 minutes

• Boil the whole **eggs** for 10 minutes, then peel.
• Beat the 2 yolks with the **mustard** and **cream cheese**. Season with salt and pepper and serve this "mayonnaise" with the cooled whole hardboiled eggs and **lettuce** leaves.

ROASTED FIGS WITH BRESAOLA

191 kcal/person

—

Gluten free

—

Lactose free

Bresaola
8 slices

Figs
x 8

Rosemary
4 small sprigs

1 drizzle olive oil

Preparation: 5 minutes
Cooking: 10 minutes

• Preheat the oven to 350°F/180°C. Make a cut in the middle of each slice of **bresaola** and slip the slices over the stem ends of the **figs**.

• Insert stem end of a sprig of **rosemary** to hold them in place and bake for 10 minutes. Serve hot with a drizzle of olive oil and an arugula salad, if desired.

STEAMED TOMATO MILLEFEUILLE

108 kcal/person

—

Vegetarian

Tomatoes
x 4 (medium)

Goat cheese
x 2 discs

Zucchini
x 1

Dried oregano
2 teaspoons (2 g)

Salt, pepper

1 drizzle olive oil

Preparation: 10 minutes
Cooking: 8 minutes

• Cut the **tomatoes**, **goat cheese**, and **zucchini** into rounds. Season with **oregano**, salt, and pepper.
• Assemble 4 millefeuilles with layers of the various ingredients. Fix in place with a wooden cocktail pick and cook for 8 minutes in a steamer.
• Transfer the millefeuilles to plates, remove the cocktail picks, sprinkle on more **oregano**, and serve warm with a drizzle of olive oil.

CAULIFLOWER, COCONUT, AND SALMON CREAM

280 kcal/person

—

Gluten free

—

Lactose free

Cauliflower
x ½

Coconut milk
1⅔ cups (400 mL)

Smoked salmon
2 slices

Grated coconut
1 tablespoon (18 g)

Preparation: 15 minutes
Cooking: 35 minutes

• Cut the **cauliflower** into small pieces. Place in a saucepan with the **coconut milk** and cook for 35 minutes over low heat. Purée with a hand blender.
• Arrange the **cauliflower** cream on four plates, cut the **smoked salmon** into pieces, and use to garnish top. Sprinkle with **grated coconut** and serve.

44

CAULIFLOWER AND SHRIMP CREAM

114 kcal/person

—

Gluten free

Cauliflower
x ½

Low-fat cream
1⅔ cups (400 mL)

Paprika
1 tablespoon (7 g)

Raw shrimp
x 20 (peeled)

Mint
1 bunch (optional)

1 drizzle olive oil

Preparation: 20 minutes
Cooking: 45 minutes

• Cut the **cauliflower** into pieces. Cook in a saucepan with the **cream** for 40 minutes over medium-high heat.
• Purée with a hand blender.
• Fry the **shrimp** for 2 minutes in a frying pan over medium-high heat with the olive oil and **paprika**.
• Arrange the **cauliflower** on plates. Add the **shrimp** and serve with **mint** sprigs, if using.

CHICKEN AND SHRIMP TERRINE

244 kcal/person

—

Gluten free

Chicken breasts
x 2

Eggs
x 2

Paprika
2 tablespoons (14 g)

Low-fat cream cheese
4 ounces (120 g)

Raw shrimp
x 16 (peeled)

 **Salt**, **pepper**

1 drizzle olive oil

Preparation: 25 minutes
Cooking: 40 minutes

• Preheat the oven to 350°F/180°C. In a blender, mix the **chicken** with the **eggs**, **paprika**, **cream cheese**, and salt and pepper.
• Cut the **shrimp** into pieces and add to the mixture. Transfer to a lightly oiled nonstick mold and bake in the oven for 40 minutes. Turn out the hot terrine and let cool. Serve with arugula, if desired.

COCKLE AND VERBENA PARCELS

50 kcal/person

—

Gluten free

—

Lactose free

Cockles
x 60 (cleaned)

Dried verbena leaves
2 pinches

Limes
x 2

🧂 **Salt, pepper**

🫗 **1 drizzle olive oil**

👥👥👥👥

⏱

Preparation: 10 minutes
Cooking: 10 minutes

• Preheat the oven to 350°F/180°C. Arrange the **cockles** and **verbena** in the center of 4 pieces of parchment paper. Season with salt and pepper. Close each parcel tightly.

• Arrange the parcels in an ovenproof dish and bake for 10 minutes. Arrange on plates and serve with **lime** wedges and a drizzle of olive oil. Discard any unopened cockles.

SALMON, AVOCADO, AND MINT TARTARE

320 kcal/person

—

Gluten free

—

Lactose free

Mint
20 leaves

Salmon fillets
14 ounces (400 g), skinless

Avocado
x 1

Lemons
x 2

Olive oil
1 tablespoon (15 mL)

 **Salt**, **pepper**

👨‍👨‍👧‍👦

⏱ **Preparation: 20 minutes**

• Roughly chop the **mint**.
• Dice the **salmon** and **avocado**. Add the juice of the **lemons**, **olive oil**, and **mint**. Season with salt and pepper, mix, and serve chilled.

STUFFED MUSHROOMS

165 kcal/person

Button mushrooms
x 8 (large)

Smoked duck breast
8 slices

Low-fat cream cheese
3½ ounces (100 g)

Soy sauce
2 tablespoons (30 mL)

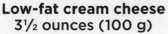
Dried thyme leaves
1 teaspoon (1 g)

 Salt, pepper

🕐
Preparation: 20 minutes
Cooking: 25 minutes

• Preheat the oven to 350°F/180°C. Remove the **mushroom** stalks and chop finely. Remove the fat from the **duck breast** and dice the meat.

• Mix the **duck** with the **cream cheese**, **thyme**, and chopped **mushroom** stalks. Season with salt and pepper. Fill the **mushroom** cups with the cream cheese mixture.

• Drizzle with **soy sauce** and bake for 25 minutes.

TROUT TARTARE

197 kcal/person

—

Gluten free

Smoked trout
4 slices

Salmon trout fillets
14 ounces (400 g), skinless

Trout roe
3½ ounces (100 g)

Plain Greek yogurt
1 tablespoon (15 g)

Lime
x 1

Preparation: 10 minutes

• Cut the **smoked trout** and **salmon trout** into small, evenly sized pieces. Mix with the **roe**, **yogurt**, and **lime** juice. Serve chilled on Swedish crispbread.

PASSION FRUIT AND SHRIMP CEVICHE

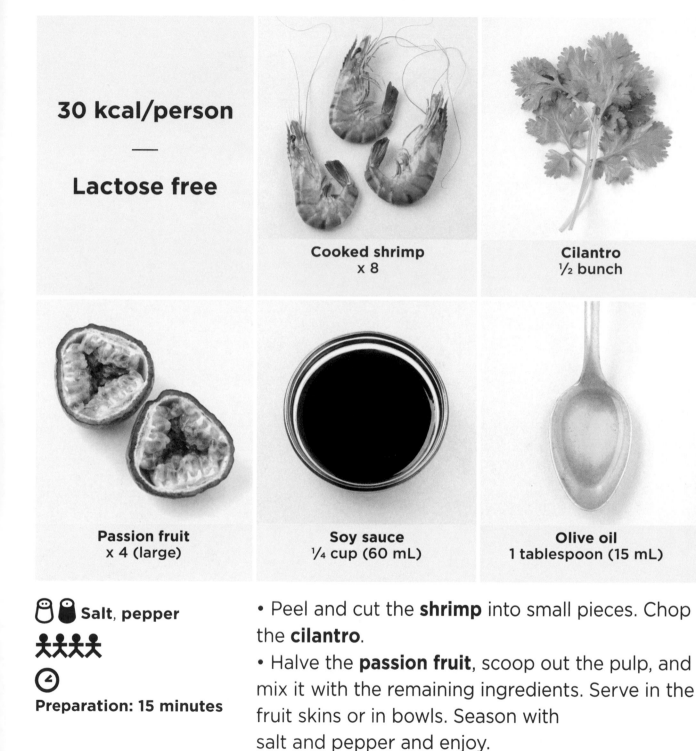

30 kcal/person

—

Lactose free

Cooked shrimp
x 8

Cilantro
½ bunch

Passion fruit
x 4 (large)

Soy sauce
¼ cup (60 mL)

Olive oil
1 tablespoon (15 mL)

Salt, pepper

Preparation: 15 minutes

• Peel and cut the **shrimp** into small pieces. Chop the **cilantro**.
• Halve the **passion fruit**, scoop out the pulp, and mix it with the remaining ingredients. Serve in the fruit skins or in bowls. Season with salt and pepper and enjoy.

LEEKS VINAIGRETTE

78 kcal/person

—

Vegetarian

—

Gluten free

Leeks
x 2

Plain Greek yogurt
10½ ounces (300 g)

Whole-grain mustard
2 tablespoons (30 g)

Chives
1 bunch

Balsamic vinegar
2 tablespoons (30 mL)

 Salt, pepper

Preparation: 15 minutes
Cooking: 40 minutes

• Cut the **leeks** in three lengthwise, then in half crosswise. Wash under cold running water and cook in a steamer for 40 minutes.
• Mix the **yogurt** with the **mustard**, chopped **chives**, and **vinegar**. Season with salt and pepper. Serve the **leeks** warm with the sauce.

SALMON IN A LEMON AND MINT MARINADE

223 kcal/person

—

Gluten free

—

Lactose free

Salmon fillets
14 ounces (400 g), skinless

Lemons
x 2

Olive oil
2 tablespoons (30 mL)

Mint
10 leaves

Salt, **pepper**

Preparation: 10 minutes
Marinating: 5 minutes

• Slice the **salmon** very thinly and arrange on small individual plates.

• Add the juice of the **lemons**, **olive oil**, and **mint**. Season with salt and pepper. Marinate for 5 minutes and serve.

ASPARAGUS MIMOSA

272 kcal/person

—

Vegetarian

—

Gluten free

Cornichons
x 16

Chervil
1 bunch

Eggs
x 2

Green asparagus
x 20

Capers
3 ounces (80 g)

 Salt, pepper

Preparation: 10 minutes
Cooking: 20 minutes

• Chop the **chervil** and **cornichons**. Boil the **eggs** for 10 minutes and peel.

• 15 minutes before serving, trim the **asparagus** and steam for 10 minutes. Place in a serving dish, and add the **chervil** and **cornichons**. Grate the **eggs** and sprinkle the **capers** over the dish. Season with salt and pepper and serve warm.

STEAMED TOMATOES FILLED WITH TUNA

73 kcal/person

—

Gluten free

Tomatoes
x 4

Low-fat cream cheese
5 ounces (150 g)

Tuna in its own juice
1 x 5.8-ounce (160 g) can

Black olives
x 16 (pitted, halved)

Dried thyme leaves
2 teaspoons (2 g)

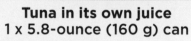
Salt, pepper

1 drizzle olive oil

👥👥👥👥

🕐

Preparation: 20 minutes
Cooking: 5 minutes

• Halve the **tomatoes** and scoop out the insides. Mix the **cream cheese** with the flaked **tuna**, **olives**, and **thyme**. Season with salt and pepper.
• Fill the **tomatoes** with the tuna mixture and cook for 5 minutes in a steamer. Serve hot or cold with a drizzle of olive oil.

MACKEREL AND TOMATOES IN WHITE WINE

90 kcal/person

—

Gluten free

—

Lactose free

Mackerel
4 fillets

Cherry tomatoes
7 ounces (200 g)

White wine
1²/₃ cups (400 mL)

Star anise
x 3

Bouquet garni
x 1

Preparation: 10 minutes
Cooking: 25 minutes
Refrigeration:
Overnight

• Preheat the oven to 350°F/180°C. Place the **mackerel** in a large gratin dish. Add the halved **tomatoes**.

• Heat the **white wine** with the **star anise**, **bouquet garni**, and about 7 tablespoons (100 mL) water for 10 minutes over medium heat. Pour the boiling liquid over the mackerel. Bake for 15 minutes. Let cool and refrigerate overnight. Serve cold.

SEA BREAM AND PINEAPPLE TARTARE

252 kcal/person

—

Gluten free

—

Lactose free

Mini pineapples
x 2

Sea bream
4 fillets (skinless)

Limes
x 2

Cilantro
1 bunch

Olive oil
2 tablespoons (30 mL)

Salt, pepper

Preparation: 20 minutes

• Cut the **pineapples** in half. Scoop out the flesh and cut into small pieces. Cut the **sea bream** into cubes. Squeeze the **limes**. Roughly chop the **coriander**. Mix all the ingredients together, season with salt and pepper, arrange in the **pineapple** halves, and serve.

MELON AND SALMON SASHIMI

330 kcal/person

—

Lactose free

Salmon steaks
x 3 (5.3 ounces or 150 g each), skinless

Cantaloupe melon
x 1 (small)

Wasabi
2 teaspoons

Soy sauce
¼ cup (60 mL)

 **Gray sea salt**

👤👤👤👤

🕐

Preparation: 10 minutes
Refrigeration:
20 minutes

• Cover the **salmon** with gray sea salt and refrigerate for 20 minutes. Rinse the **salmon** in cold water and cut into pieces.
• Peel the **melon** and cut into pieces the same size as the **salmon**. Arrange together in a serving dish.
• Mix 1 teaspoon of the **wasabi** with the **soy sauce**, pour over, and serve. Garnish with remaining wasabi.

OYSTERS WITH MANDARIN JUICE AND BASIL

137 kcal/person

—

Lactose free

Mandarins
x 6

Oysters
x 24 (small)

Basil
24 leaves

Olive oil
24 drops

Soy sauce
24 drops

 **24 pinches pepper**

Gray sea salt

Preparation: 10 minutes
Cooking: 5 minutes

• Preheat the oven to 350°F/180°C. Squeeze the **mandarins** and reserve the juice.
• Bake **oysters** for 5 minutes. Allow to cool before opening. Pour off the liquor and arrange the **oysters** on a bed of sea salt. Refrigerate.
• Two minutes before serving, put a **basil** leaf on each **oyster**. Add **mandarin** juice, **olive oil**, **soy sauce**, and pepper to each oyster.

OYSTERS WITH MANGO AND CILANTRO

108 kcal/person

—

Lactose free

Shallot
x 1 (or 2 small)

Mango
x ½ (not too ripe)

Cilantro
6 sprigs

Oysters
x 24 (small)

Cider vinegar
24 drops

Gray sea salt

24 drops olive oil

Preparation: 10 minutes
Cooking: 5 minutes

• Preheat the oven to 350°F/180°C. Dice the **shallot** and **mango**. Chop the **cilantro**. Bake the **oysters** for 5 minutes. Let cool before opening. Pour off the **oyster** liquor and arrange the **oysters** on a bed of sea salt. Refrigerate.

• Mix together the **mango**, **shallot**, olive oil, **vinegar**, and **cilantro**. Top the **oysters** with it.

CAESAR SALAD

351 kcal/person

Little Gem lettuces
x 4

Chicken breasts
1 pound, 5 ounces (600 g)

Swedish crispbread
2 slices

Plain Greek yogurt
¼ cup (60 g)

Grated Parmesan cheese
¼ cup (25 g)

 Salt, pepper

Preparation: 10 minutes
Cooking: 20 minutes

• Cook the **chicken breasts** for 20 minutes in a steamer or in simmering water. Cut into pieces. Separate the **lettuce** leaves.

• Break the **crispbread** into pieces.

• Mix all ingredients in a salad bowl. Season with salt and pepper and serve.

EGGPLANT SALAD

79 kcal/person

—

Vegan

—

Gluten free

Eggplants
x 2 (medium)

Tomatoes
x 3

Black olives
x 20 (pitted)

Basil
1 bunch

Olive oil
2 tablespoons (30 mL)

Salt, pepper

Preparation: 10 minutes
Cooking: 40 minutes

• Cook the **eggplants** whole for 40 minutes in a steamer and let cool.

• Cut the **tomatoes** and **olives** into pieces and chop the **basil**. Cut open the **eggplants**, scoop out the flesh with a spoon, and mix with the other ingredients. Season with salt and pepper and serve.

BEEF, MÂCHE, AND TURMERIC SALAD

192 kcal/person

—

Gluten Free

Filet of beef
14 ounces (400 g)

Mâche
5 ounces (150 g)

Plain Greek yogurt
5 ounces (150 g)

Turmeric
1 tablespoon (7 g)

 **Salt**, **pepper**

Preparation: 15 minutes
Cooking: 8 minutes

• Cook the **beef** for 8 minutes in a steamer. Let cool, cut the meat into thin slices, and mix with the **mâche**, **yogurt**, and **turmeric**. Season with salt and pepper and serve.

BROCCOLI AND DRIED FRUIT SALAD

60 kcal/person

—

Vegan

Broccoli
1 pound (445 g)

Slivered almonds
2 tablespoons (14 g)

Dried apricots
x 8

Walnut halves
x 8

Hazelnuts
x 16

Salt, pepper

1 drizzle hazelnut oil

Preparation: 15 minutes
Cooking: 10 minutes

• Cut the **broccoli** into pieces and cook for 10 minutes in a steamer. Cut the **apricots** into pieces, and chop the **walnuts** and **hazelnuts**.
• In a salad bowl, mix the **broccoli** with the **almonds**, **apricots**, **walnuts**, and **hazelnuts**. Season with salt and pepper. Serve with a drizzle of hazelnut oil.

LENTIL AND SHRIMP SALAD

230 kcal/person

—

Gluten free

—

Lactose free

Green lentils
9 ounces (250 g)

Cooked shrimp
x 16 (peeled)

Clementines
x 4

Tarragon
1 bunch

Olive oil
2 tablespoons (30 mL)

 **Salt, pepper**

**Preparation: 15 minutes
Cooking: 25 minutes**

• Cook the **lentils** for 25 minutes in a large quantity of water. Drain, transfer to a salad bowl, and let cool.
• Add the **shrimp**, cut into pieces, the juice of the **clementines**, the chopped **tarragon**, and the **olive oil**. Season with salt and pepper, mix, and serve.

PINEAPPLE AND CHICKEN SALAD

334 kcal/person

—

Gluten free

Chicken breasts
x 3

Mini pineapple
x 1

Arugula
5 ounces (150 g)

Plain Greek yogurt
5 ounces (150 g)

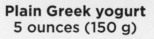
Cider vinegar
1 tablespoon (15 mL)

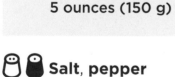 **Salt, pepper**

**Preparation: 15 minutes
Cooking: 20 minutes**

• Cook the **chicken breasts** for 20 minutes in a steamer or in simmering water. Let cool and cut into pieces.

• Skin the **pineapple** and cut into cubes. Mix all the ingredients together in a salad bowl. Season with salt and pepper and serve immediately.

BEEF SALAD WITH RASPBERRIES

191 kcal/person

—

Gluten free

Raspberries
4½ ounces (125 g)

Filet or rib steak
14 ounces (400 g)

Arugula
4¼ ounces (120 g)

Balsamic vinegar
2 tablespoons (30 mL)

Plain Greek yogurt
150 g (30 mL)

 **Salt**, pepper

Preparation: 20 minutes
Cooking: 30 seconds

• Halve the **raspberries**.
• Cut the **steak** into cubes and sear for 30 seconds in a very hot dry pan, stirring continuously.
• Put the **arugula** in a salad bowl with half the **vinegar** and the **yogurt**. Mix and arrange on a serving plate. Add the **steak**, **raspberries**, and remaining **vinegar** and **yogurt** to the bowl. Season with salt and pepper, mix, and serve immediately.

VEAL SALAD WITH BLUEBERRIES

160 kcal/person

—

Gluten free

Veal escalopes
x 2

Blueberries
4½ ounces (125 g)

Plain Greek yogurt
5 ounces (150 g)

Arugula
4 ounces (120 g)

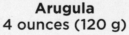
Mustard
1 tablespoon (15 g)

Salt, pepper

Preparation: 15 minutes
Cooking: 1 minute

• Cut the **veal** into small pieces and sear for 1 minute in a very hot dry pan, stirring continuously.

• Put the **veal** in a salad bowl with the other ingredients. Season with salt and pepper, mix, and serve immediately.

APPLES WITH HOT GOAT CHEESE

325 kcal/person

—

Vegetarian

—

Gluten free

Apples
x 2

Goat cheese
x 2 discs

Honey
2 tablespoons (40 g)

Walnut halves
x 12

Arugula
3½ ounces (100 g)

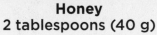**1 drizzle walnut oil**

Preparation: 10 minutes
Cooking: 15 minutes

• Preheat the oven to 350°F/180°C. Peel the **apples**, halve, and remove the cores. Put half a **cheese** disc (sliced horizontally) on each **apple** half, cover with **honey**, and bake for 15 minutes.
• Chop the **walnuts**. Arrange the hot **cheese** and **apple** on a bed of **arugula**, add the **walnuts**, and serve with a drizzle of walnut oil.

OCTOPUS SALAD

213 kcal/person

—

Gluten free

—

Lactose free

Limes
x 2

Cilantro
2 bunches

Octopus
x 1 (about 2 pounds, or 1 kg)

Paprika
1 tablespoon (15 g)

Olive oil
2 tablespoons (30 mL)

Preparation: 15 minutes
Cooking: 20 minutes

• Squeeze the **limes** and chop the **cilantro**.
• Place the **octopus** in a casserole, cover with water, and bring to the boil. Cook for 20 minutes, then take off the heat. Leave to cool in the casserole.
• Cut the **octopus** into pieces and mix with the remaining ingredients. Serve immediately with additional lime wedges, if desired.

GREEN TOMATOES WITH MOZZARELLA

175 kcal/person

—

Vegetarian

—

Gluten free

Basil
2 bunches

Green tomatoes
x 4

Mozzarella cheese
5 ounces (150 g)

Pine nuts
2 tablespoons (18 g)

Salt, pepper

1 drizzle olive oil

Preparation: 10 minutes
Cooking: 10 minutes

• Preheat the oven to 350°F/180°C. Chop the **basil**.
• Halve the **tomatoes** and place a piece of **mozzarella** on each half. Bake for 10 minutes.
• Arrange the **tomatoes** in a serving dish. Add the **basil** and **pine nuts**, season with salt and pepper, and serve warm with a drizzle of olive oil.

GRATED CARROTS WITH CILANTRO

47 kcal/person

—

Vegetarian

—

Lactose free

Cilantro
1 bunch

Clementines
x 2

Carrots
3 (large, about
1 pound, or 445 g)

Soy sauce
3 tablespoons (45 mL)

 **Salt**, pepper

♟♟♟♟

🕐
Preparation: 15 minutes

• Chop the **cilantro**. Squeeze the **clementines**.
• Grate the **carrots** and mix with the remaining ingredients. Season with salt and pepper and serve.

TOMATO SALAD WITH HERBS

94 kcal/person

—

Vegetarian

—

Gluten free

Basil
1 bunch

Tarragon
1 bunch

Low-fat cream cheese
4½ ounces (120 g)

Tomatoes
x 9 (medium), red and green

 **Salt**, pepper

Preparation: **15 minutes**

• Pick off the **basil** and **tarragon** leaves. In a blender, mix three-fourths of the herbs with the **cream cheese** and 4 teaspoons (20 mL) water.

• Mix this sauce with the **tomatoes**, cut into pieces. Add the remaining herbs. Season with salt and pepper and serve.

BRUSSELS SPROUT SALAD

145 kcal/person

—

Gluten free

Bresaola
4 thin slices

Hazelnuts
x 12

Brussels sprouts
x 24

Hazelnut oil
1 tablespoon (15 mL)

 **Salt, pepper**

Preparation: 15 minutes
Cooking: 15 minutes

• Cut the **bresaola** into small strips. Roughly chop the **hazelnuts**.

• Steam the **Brussels sprouts** for 15 minutes. Halve them and mix with the **bresaola** strips and **hazelnuts**, drizzle with **hazelnut oil**, season with salt and pepper, and serve hot or cold.

MUSSEL SALAD

360 kcal/person

—

Gluten free

—

Lactose free

Mussels
3 quarts (3 L), cleaned and debearded

Peas
10½ ounces (300 g)

Cucumber
9 ounces (250 g)

Mâche
5 ounces (150 g)

 **Salt, pepper**

1 drizzle olive oil

Preparation: 20 minutes
Cooking: 15 minutes

• Place the **mussels** in a saucepan over high heat and stir continuously until they open. Strain and reserve any cooking juices. Remove **mussels** from shells.

• In a blender, blend three-fourths of the **peas**, the olive oil, half the **cucumber**, and the cooking juices.

• Mix everything together with the remaining **cucumber**, peeled and sliced, the **peas**, and the **mâche**. Season with salt and pepper.

CAULIFLOWER TABBOULEH

43 kcal/person

—

Vegetarian

Mint
1 bunch

Cauliflower
x 1

Cucumber
9 ounces (250 g)

Tomatoes
x 2

 Salt, pepper

Preparation: 15 minutes
Cooking: 10 minutes

• Chop the **mint**.
• Remove the stalk and leaves of the **cauliflower** and grate the **cauliflower** by hand. Place on a sheet of moistened parchment paper and cook for 10 minutes in a steamer.
• Mix the **cauliflower** "couscous" with the diced **cucumber**, **tomatoes**, and **mint**. Season with salt and pepper and serve.

PEA GAZPACHO

92 kcal/person

—

Vegetarian

—

Lactose free

Mint
1 bunch

Peas
1 pound (445 g), fresh or frozen

Cucumber
14 ounces (400 g)

Olive oil
12 drops

 **Salt**, pepper

Preparation: 20 minutes
Cooking: 5 minutes

• Chop the **mint**.
• Cook the **peas** for 5 minutes in boiling water. Drain.
• In a blender, mix the **peas** with the **cucumber**, about 7 tablespoons (100 mL) water, and the **olive oil**. Season with salt and pepper, add the mint, and serve chilled.

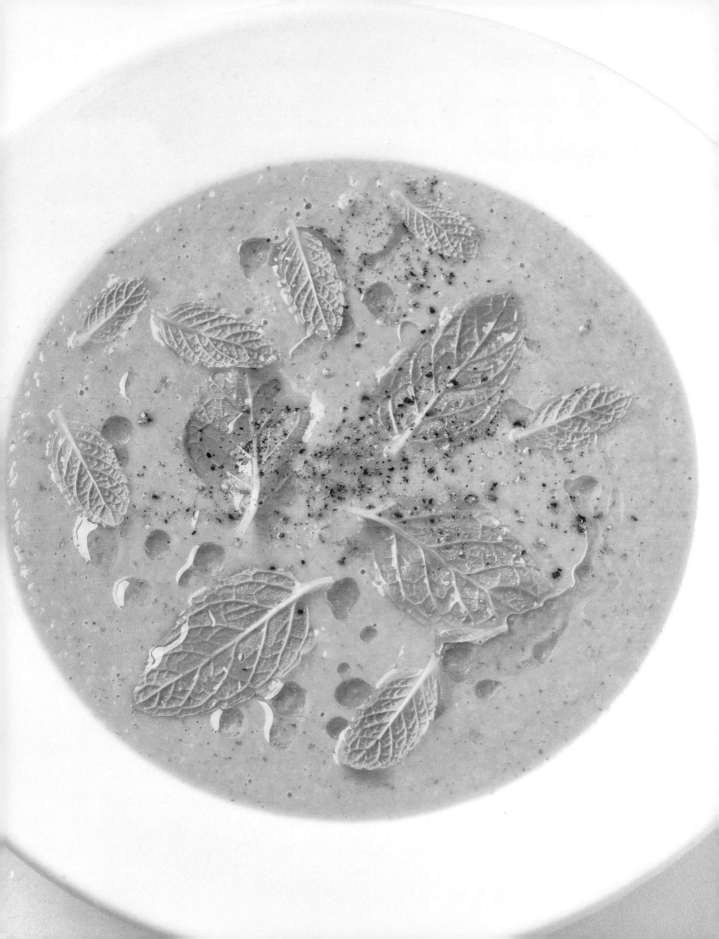

ARTICHOKE AND CUCUMBER GAZPACHO

130 kcal/person

—

Vegetarian

—

Lactose free

Cucumber
14 ounces (400 g)

Artichoke bottoms
x 8

Olive oil
2 tablespoons (30 mL)

Salt, pepper

1 drizzle olive oil

Preparation: 10 minutes
Cooking: 30 minutes

• Dice the **cucumber**. Cook the **artichoke bottoms** for 30 minutes in boiling salted water. Drain and let cool.

• Blend the **artichoke bottoms** with half the **cucumber**, 3 tablespoons plus 1 teaspoon (50 mL) water, and the **olive oil**.

• Season with salt and pepper and pour into bowls. Add the remaining diced **cucumber** and serve chilled. Garnish with additional olive oil.

MELON, TOMATO, AND MINT GAZPACHO

110 kcal/person

—

Gluten free

—

Lactose free

Mint
1 bunch

Tomatoes
x 4 (medium)

Cantaloupe melon
x 1

Olive oil
2 tablespoons (30 mL)

Salt, pepper

Preparation: 10 minutes

• Chop the **mint** (reserve a few small leaves). Halve the **tomatoes**, scoop out the insides, and chop. Peel and seed the **melon**.

• In a blender, mix the **melon**, **tomatoes**, **mint**, 4 teaspoons (20 mL) water, and the **olive oil**. Season with salt and pepper and refrigerate.

• Transfer to bowls, add the reserved **mint** leaves, and serve.

WATERMELON AND TOMATO GAZPACHO

98 kcal/person

—

Vegetarian

—

Gluten free

Mint
1 bunch

Grape tomatoes
9 ounces (250 g), red and yellow

Watermelon
2 pounds (900 g)

Salt, **pepper**

1 drizzle olive oil

Preparation: 10 minutes

• Chop the **mint** (reserve a few small leaves). Halve the **tomatoes**. Seed and chop the **watermelon**.

• In a blender, mix the **watermelon** with three-fourths of the **tomatoes**, 4 teaspoons (20 mL) water, and the **mint**. Season and refrigerate.

• Transfer the gazpacho to bowls. Add the remaining **tomatoes**, **mint** leaves, and a drizzle of olive oil.

MELON, FETA, AND OREGANO GAZPACHO

175 kcal/person

—

Vegetarian

—

Gluten free

Cantaloupe melons
x 2

Feta cheese
3½ ounces (100 g)

Dried oregano
4 teaspoons (4 g)

🧂🧂 Salt, pepper

🫙 1 drizzle olive oil

👪

🕐

Preparation: 10 minutes

• Peel and seed the **melons**. Cut about ¼ cup (40 g) of flesh into small cubes. Crush the **feta** with a fork.

• In a blender, mix the remaining **melon** flesh with 3 tablespoons plus 1 teaspoon (50 mL) water and the **oregano**. Season with salt and pepper and refrigerate.

• Transfer the gazpacho to bowls. Add the **feta**, **melon** cubes, and a drizzle of olive oil. Serve chilled.

VEGETABLE BOUILLON WITH SALMON

167 kcal/person

—

Gluten free

—

Lactose free

Carrots
10½ ounces (300 g)

Celeriac
10½ ounces (300 g)

Peas
5 ounces (150 g)

Button mushrooms
3½ ounces (100 g)

Salmon steaks
x 2 (skinless)

Preparation: 15 minutes
Cooking: 45 minutes

• Peel and dice the **carrots** and **celeriac**. Cook for 45 minutes over low heat in 1½ quarts (1.5 L) water. Add the **peas** halfway through cooking.

• Cut the **mushrooms** and **salmon** into small pieces and arrange together in bowls. Pour the piping hot bouillon over and let stand for 1 minute before serving.

GREEN TEA, SALMON, AND GRAPEFRUIT

180 kcal/person

—

Gluten free

—

Lactose free

Salmon fillets
9 ounces (250 g), skinless

Pink grapefruit
x 2

Jasmine green tea
1²/₃ cups (400 mL), cold

Kiwi
x 2

Cilantro
12 sprigs

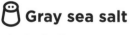 **Gray sea salt**

♙♙♙♙

🕐

Preparation: 20 minutes
Refrigeration:
40 minutes

• Cover the **salmon** with coarse gray sea salt. Refrigerate for 40 minutes.
• Squeeze the **grapefruit** to give 6¾ fluid ounces (200 mL) juice. Mix with the **tea**.
• Rinse the **salmon** in cold water and cut into cubes. Divide into bowls and top with the chopped **kiwi** and **cilantro**. Cover with the tea and juice mixture and serve.

BEEF BOUILLON WITH LEMONGRASS

185 kcal/person

—

Lactose free

Napa cabbage
14 ounces (400 g)

Lemongrass
2 stalks

Broccoli
3½ ounces (100 g)

Zucchini
x 1

Filet of beef
14 ounces (400 g)

 **1 drizzle soy sauce**

Preparation: 15 minutes
Cooking: 40 minutes

• Cook the thinly sliced **napa cabbage**, sliced **lemongrass**, chopped **broccoli**, and the **zucchini**, cut into rounds, in a saucepan with 1½ quarts (1.5 L) water for 40 minutes over low heat.

• Cut the **beef** into small cubes and divide among 4 bowls. Pour the piping hot bouillon over and let stand for 1 minute, or until your desired doneness. Serve with a drizzle of soy sauce.

BUTTERNUT SQUASH SOUP WITH WALNUTS

80 kcal/person

—

Vegetarian

—

Lactose free

Butternut squash
x 1 (1 pound 5 ounces, or
about 600 g)

Carrots
x 2

Sweet onion
x 1

Walnut halves
x 8

Walnut oil
1 tablespoon (15 mL)

 **Salt, pepper**

👤👤👤👤

🕐

Preparation: 20 minutes
Cooking: 45 minutes

• Peel the **squash**, **carrots**, and **onion** and cut into big chunks. Place in a casserole, add enough water to cover by ½ inch (1 cm) and cook for 45 minutes over low heat. Purée with a hand blender.

• Season with salt and pepper and transfer to bowls. Add the chopped **walnuts** and a few drops of **walnut oil** to each bowl and serve.

BEEF BOUILLON WITH TEA

138 kcal/person

—

Gluten free

—

Lactose free

Filet of beef
7 ounces (200 g)

Green asparagus
x 8

Cucumber
3½ ounces (100 g)

Basil
20 leaves

Earl Grey tea
1⅔ cups (400 mL), hot

 Gray sea salt

Preparation: 10 minutes
Refrigeration:
40 minutes

• Cover the **beef** with coarse gray sea salt. Refrigerate for 40 minutes.
• Trim the **asparagus** and cut into small cubes. Dice the **cucumber**.
• Rinse the **beef** in cold water. Cut into cubes and divide into bowls with the **asparagus**, **cucumber**, and chopped **basil**. Pour the boiling hot **tea** over, let stand for 1 minute, or until your desired doneness, and serve.

BEEF AND CARROT BOUILLON

130 kcal/person

—

Gluten free

—

Lactose free

Carrots
1 pound (445 g)

Turnips
9 ounces (250 g)

Filet of beef
9 ounces (250 g)

Tarragon
1 bunch

 **Salt, pepper**

**Preparation: 10 minutes
Cooking: 45 minutes**

• Cut the **carrots** and **turnips** into small evenly sized cubes and cook for 45 minutes over low heat in 1 quart (1 L) water. Remove from the heat and add the **beef**, cut into small pieces.

• Let stand for 5 minutes in the hot bouillon. Season with salt and pepper, add the chopped **tarragon,** and serve.

RATATOUILLE AND CHORIZO BOUILLON

53 kcal/person

—

Gluten free

—

Lactose free

Red bell pepper
x 1

Tomatoes
x 2

Basil
1 bunch

Chorizo
4 thin slices

Zucchini
x 2

Salt, **pepper**

👨👨👨👨

🕐
Preparation: 25 minutes
Cooking: 45 minutes

• Seed and dice the **red bell pepper** and **tomatoes**. Cook for 45 minutes over low heat in a casserole with 1½ quarts (1.5 L) water.
• Chop the **basil**, cut the **chorizo** into strips, and chop the **zucchini**. Mix the **basil**, **chorizo**, and **zucchini** into the bouillon. Season with salt and pepper and serve.

TURKEY BOUILLON WITH FENNEL

138 kcal/person

—

Gluten free

—

Lactose free

Turkey escalopes
x 3 (5 ounces, or 150 g each)

Fennel
2 bulbs

Grape tomatoes
x 20, red and yellow

Fennel seeds
1 tablespoon (6 g)

Dill
1 bunch

 Salt, pepper

Preparation: 20 minutes
Cooking: 1 hour

• Cut the **turkey escalopes** into small pieces. Cut the **fennel** into pieces and place with the **turkey** in a casserole with 1½ quarts (1.5 L) water. Bring to a simmer, cover, and cook over low heat for a half hour.
• Add the **cherry tomatoes** and **fennel seeds** 10 minutes before the end of cooking time. Season and transfer to bowls. Add the chopped **dill**, let stand for 1 minute, and serve.

SCALLOP BOUILLON WITH CELERY

44 kcal/person

—

Gluten free

—

Lactose free

Celery
1 stalk

Lemongrass
2 stalks

Pink grapefruit
x 2

Fresh baby spinach
3½ ounces (100 g)

Scallops
x 12

Salt, pepper

Preparation: 20 minutes
Cooking: 25 minutes

• Trim and slice the **celery** and slice the **lemongrass**. Cook for 25 minutes in 1½ quarts (1.5 L) water over low heat. Squeeze the **grapefruit** and strain the juice.

• Remove the stems from the **spinach** leaves. Add to the bouillon with the **scallops**. Remove from heat and let cool. Add the **grapefruit** juice, season with salt and pepper, and serve.

THAI SOUP WITH CHICKEN AND SHRIMP

600 kcal/person

—

Gluten free

—

Lactose free

Chicken breasts
x 2

Button mushrooms
1 pound (455 g)

Lemongrass
2 stalks

Coconut milk
27 fluid ounces (800 mL)

Raw shrimp
x 12 (peeled)

Salt, pepper

Preparation: 25 minutes
Cooking: 46 minutes

• Cut the **chicken** and **mushrooms** into pieces and slice the **lemongrass**. Cook in a casserole with the **coconut milk** for 45 minutes over low heat.
• Add the **shrimp** and cook for 1 minute more. Season with salt and pepper.

FISH CONSOMMÉ WITH GREEN TEA

140 kcal/person

—

Gluten free

—

Lactose free

Cod
12 ounces (350 g)

Black olives
x 12 (pitted)

Tarragon
1 bunch

Clementines
x 4

Jasmine green tea
17 fluid ounces (500 mL),
cold

Preparation: 10 minutes
Cooking: 5 minutes

• Steam or boil the **cod** for 5 minutes. Divide it among 4 bowls. Add the **olives**, chopped, and the chopped **tarragon**.

• Mix the strained **clementine** juice with the cold **tea**. Pour into the bowls and serve.

SHRIMP BOUILLON WITH GINGER

64 kcal/person

—

Lactose free

Napa cabbage
14 ounces (400 g)

Fresh ginger
1¾ ounces (50 g)

Aniseed
2 tablespoons (13 g)

Raw shrimp
x 24 (peeled)

Soy sauce
¼ cup (60 mL)

Preparation: 20 minutes
Cooking: 46 minutes

• In a casserole, cook the thinly sliced **napa cabbage**, the **ginger**, peeled and cut into thin rounds, and the **aniseed** in 1½ quarts (1.5 L) water for 45 minutes over low heat.

• Add the **shrimp** and **soy sauce**. Cook for 1 minute more and serve.

CREAMY SALMON AND SPINACH SOUP

435 kcal/person

—

Gluten free

—

Lactose free

Fresh baby spinach
10½ ounces (300 g)

Coconut milk
3⅓ cups (800 mL)

Celeriac
5 ounces (150 g)

Smoked salmon
4 slices

Salt, pepper

Preparation: 20 minutes
Cooking: 20 minutes

• Trim the **spinach** and reserve about 40 small leaves. Cook for 20 minutes over low heat in a casserole with the **coconut milk**, the **celeriac** cut into pieces, and 17 flud ounces (500 mL) water.
• Purée with a hand blender. Season with salt and pepper and arrange in bowls. Add the **spinach** and **salmon**, cut into small pieces. Serve with garnish.

VEGETABLE MINESTRONE

64 kcal/person

—

Vegetarian

—

Gluten free

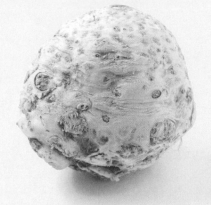

Celeriac
10½ ounces (300 g)

Carrots
10½ ounces (300 g)

Green beans
3½ ounces (100 g)

Peas
5 ounces (150 g)

Cherry tomatoes
x 8

 **Salt**, pepper

A few drops olive oil

Preparation: 20 minutes
Cooking: 50 minutes

• Peel and dice the **celeriac** and **carrots** and cut the **green beans** into small pieces. Cook for 45 minutes over low heat in 1½ quarts (1.5 L) water.

• Add the **peas** and the halved **tomatoes** and cook for 5 minutes more. Season with salt and pepper and serve with a few drops of olive oil.

CHICKEN BOUILLON WITH GINGER

282 kcal/person

—

Lactose free

Chicken breasts
x 3

Fresh ginger
3 ounces (80 g)

Cherry tomatoes
9 ounces (250 g)

Basil
1 bunch

Soy sauce
¼ cup (60 mL)

Preparation: 20 minutes
Cooking: 45 minutes

• In a casserole, cook the **chicken**, cut into pieces, the peeled and grated **ginger**, and the halved **tomatoes** in 1½ quarts (1.5 L) water for 45 minutes over low heat.

• Pick off and chop the **basil** leaves. Add to the bouillon with the **soy sauce**. Mix and serve.

148

CABBAGE SOUP WITH HADDOCK

175 kcal/person

—

Gluten free

—

Lactose free

Sweet onion
x 1

Savoy cabbage
1 pound (445 g)

Carrots
x 2

Bouquet garni
x 1

Haddock
1 fillet (12 ounces or 350 g)

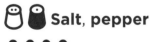 **Salt**, pepper

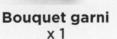

**Preparation: 15 minutes
Cooking: 1 hour**

• In a casserole, cook the thinly sliced **onion**, the **cabbage**, cut into pieces, the **carrots**, cut into rounds, and the **bouquet garni** in 1½ quarts (1.5 L) water for 55 minutes over low heat.

• Add the **haddock**, cut into pieces, and cook for 5 minutes more. Season with salt and pepper and serve.

SCALLOPS IN VANILLA BOUILLON

52 kcal/person

—

Gluten free

—

Lactose free

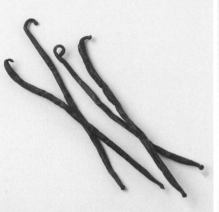
Vanilla
3 beans

Pink grapefruit
x 1

Leeks
x 2 (small)

Scallops
x 12 (with or without coral)

Preparation: 15 minutes
Cooking: 23 minutes

• Split the **vanilla** beans lengthwise. Scrape and reserve the seeds. Squeeze the **grapefruit** and strain about 7 tablespoons (100 mL) juice.

• Wash the **leeks**, slice thinly, and cook with the sliced **vanilla beans** in 1½ quarts (1.5 L) water for 15 minutes over low heat. Add the **scallops**, cut into pieces, and cook for 8 minutes more. Serve in bowls, topped with the **grapefruit** juice and **vanilla** seeds.

AVOCADO AND PEAR BOUILLON

162 kcal/person

—

Vegetarian

—

Gluten free

Pink grapefruit
x 2

Green tea with lemon
1½ quarts (1.5 mL), cold

Pears
x 2

Avocado
x 1

Basil
16 leaves

Pepper

Preparation: 20 minutes

• Squeeze the **grapefruit** and strain the juice to give 6¾ fluid ounces (200 mL); mix this with the cold **tea**.

• Just before serving, cut the **pears** and **avocado** into pieces, trim the **basil**, and arrange in bowls. Add the **tea** and **grapefruit** juice mixture, season lightly with pepper, and serve.

CREAM OF ARTICHOKE WITH SOFTBOILED EGGS

217 kcal/person

—

Gluten free

Artichoke bottoms
x 8

Low-fat cream cheese
4¼ ounces (120 g)

Bresaola
4 slices

Eggs
x 4

Salt, pepper

Preparation: 15 minutes
Cooking: 35 minutes

• Cook the **artichoke bottoms** for 30 minutes in boiling salted water. Drain. In a blender, mix the cooked artichokes with the **cream cheese** and 3 tablespoons plus 1 teaspoon (50 mL) water. Season with salt and pepper.

• Cut **bresaola** into thin strips. Boil the **eggs** for exactly 5 minutes then peel under cold running water.

• Transfer the **artichoke** cream to plates. Add the **beef** strips and the halved **eggs**.

BEEF BOUILLON WITH MUSHROOMS

117 kcal/person

—

Gluten free

—

Lactose free

Turnips
7 ounces (200 g)

Carrots
9 ounces (250 g)

Thyme
1 tablespoon (2.45 g)

Button mushrooms
5 ounces (150 g)

Filet or rib steak
7 ounces (200 g)

Preparation: 15 minutes
Cooking: 45 minutes

• In a casserole, cook the diced **turnips**, diced **carrots**, and **thyme** in 1½ quarts (1.5 L) water for 45 minutes over low heat.

• Cut the **mushrooms** and **steak** into small pieces and divide among 4 bowls. Pour the piping hot bouillon over, let stand for 1 minute, or until your desired doneness, and serve.

CREAM OF SPINACH, CELERY, AND SHRIMP

217 kcal/person

—

Gluten free

—

Lactose free

Fresh spinach
3½ ounces (100 g)

Celery
2 stalks

Coconut milk
1⅔ cups (400 mL)

Raw shrimp
x 16 (peeled)

Cilantro
12 sprigs

 **Salt, pepper**

Preparation: 10 minutes
Cooking: 47 minutes

• In a soup pot, cook the **spinach** and chopped **celery** for 45 minutes over low heat with the **coconut milk** and about 7 tablespoons (100 mL) water. Purée with a hand blender and season with salt and pepper.

• Add the **shrimp** and cook for 2 minutes more. Transfer to bowls, add the **cilantro**, and serve.

SEAFOOD WITH GREEN TEA

131 kcal/person

—

Gluten free

—

Lactose free

Oysters
x 12 (medium)

Jasmine green tea
17 fluid ounces (500 mL)

Lemon thyme
4 sprigs

Cooked shrimp
x 12

Cherry tomatoes
x 8

Preparation: 15 minutes
Cooking: 10 minutes

• Preheat the oven to 350°F/180°C. Bake the **oysters** for 5 minutes. Open them and divide among 4 bowls. Mix the liquor from the **oysters** with the **tea** and **thyme**. Heat and let stand for 5 minutes, strain, and let cool.

• Peel the **shrimp** and add to the bowls along with the chopped **tomatoes**. Pour the **tea** over and serve.

DUCK BOUILLON WITH SAGE

66 kcal/person

—

Lactose free

Button mushrooms
1 pound, 5 ounces (600 g)

Sage
18 leaves

Duck fillets
x 4

Soy sauce
¼ cup (60 mL)

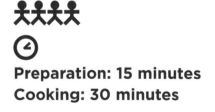

Preparation: 15 minutes
Cooking: 30 minutes

• Thinly slice the **mushrooms** and trim the **sage**. Place in a saucepan, add 1½ quarts (1.5 L) water, and cook for 30 minutes over low heat.
• Slice the **duck** into thin strips and divide into bowls with the **soy sauce**. Pour the piping hot bouillon over, let stand for 1 minute, and serve.

TARTAR SAUCE

44 kcal/person

To serve with:

Poached or steamed fish
Grilled meat or fish
Grated red or white cabbage
Steamed vegetables
Poached or steamed poultry
Raw vegetable sticks
Omelets
Salads

Low-fat cream cheese
4¼ ounces (120 g)

Mustard
1 tablespoon (15 g)

Capers
2 ounces (60 g)

Tarragon
1 bunch

Chives
1 bunch

Salt, pepper

Preparation: 15 minutes

• Mix together the **cream cheese**, **mustard**, and roughly chopped **capers**.

• Stir in the chopped **tarragon** and **chives**. Season with salt and pepper and serve.

SAUCE VIERGE

94 kcal/person

___

To serve with:

Meat

Fish

Grilled poultry

Steamed vegetables

Salads

Raw vegetables

Steamed fish, shellfish, or poultry

White beans

Lentils

Oranges
x 4

Cucumber
x 1 (7 ounces, or 200 g)

Tomatoes
x 2

Basil
1 bunch

Soy sauce
¼ cup (60 mL)

 **Salt, pepper**

Preparation: 15 minutes

• Squeeze the **oranges**. Cut the **cucumber** and **tomatoes** into small cubes. Pick off the **basil** leaves and chop.

• Mix all the ingredients with the **orange juice** and **soy sauce**. Season with salt and pepper and serve.

AÏOLI

42 kcal/person

To serve with:
Steamed or boiled vegetables
Grilled meat, fish, or poultry
Steamed fish, shellfish, or poultry
Whole-grain pasta
Brown rice
Baked potatoes

Garlic
15 cloves

Saffron threads
1 heaping teaspoon (1 g)

Plain Greek yogurt
4¼ ounces (120 g)

Salt, pepper

Preparation: 15 minutes
Cooking: 30 minutes

• Peel the **garlic** cloves and remove the green germs. Cook in 6¾ fluid ounces (200 mL) water for about 30 minutes over low heat or until tender enough to be crushed with a fork. Remove from the heat and let cool.

• Add the **saffron** and **yogurt** to the crushed **garlic**. Purée with a hand blender. Season with salt and pepper and serve.

RED WINE SAUCE

108 kcal/person

To serve with:
Grilled meat, fish, or poultry
Poached or boiled eggs
Steamed vegetables
Seafood
Fried Brussels sprouts
Tofu

Shallots
x 6

Garlic
2 cloves

Red wine
2 cups (480 mL)

Beef stock
1¼ cups (300 mL)

Bouquets garnis
x 2

Salt, pepper

Preparation: 15 minutes
Cooking: 1 hour

• Peel the **shallots** and **garlic**, slice thinly, and place in a saucepan with the **red wine**, **stock**, and **bouquets garnis**.

• Cook over low heat for about 1 hour until the sauce is reduced by one-fourth and thickens. Season with salt and pepper and serve hot.

RAVIGOTE SAUCE

109 kcal/person

To serve with:
Artichoke bottoms
Canned salsify
Poached chicken
Steamed quenelles
Lettuce or chicory hearts
Roasts
Tomato salad
Meat
Grilled fish

Parsley
1 bunch

Low-fat cream cheese
6 ounces (180 g)

Cornichons
x 16

Eggs
2 (hardboiled)

Strong mustard
1 tablespoon (15 g)

Preparation: 15 minutes

• Pick off the **parsley** leaves and chop. Mix with the **cream cheese**, chopped **cornichons**, crushed hardboiled **eggs**, and **mustard**.

BOLOGNESE SAUCE

123 kcal/person

—

To serve with:
Steamed vegetables
Palm hearts
Whole-grain pasta
Green cabbage
Cauliflower
Brussels sprouts
Zucchini rounds

Turkey escalopes
x 2 (5 ounces, or 150 g each)

Tomatoes
1 pound (445 g), ripe

Sweet onion
x 1

Tomato purée
2 tablespoons (30 g)

Dried thyme leaves
1 tablespoon (3 g)

 **Salt**, **pepper**

👤👤👤👤

🕐

Preparation: 15 minutes
Cooking: 45 minutes

• Cut the **turkey escalopes** into cubes and the **tomatoes** and **onion** into small pieces. Cook with the **tomato purée** and **thyme** in 6 ¾ fluid ounces (200 mL) water for 45 minutes over low heat.
• Purée with a hand blender. Season with salt and pepper and serve.

CARBONARA SAUCE

152 kcal/person

To serve with:
Steamed vegetables
Palm hearts
Whole-grain pasta
Brussels sprouts
Zucchini rounds

Low-fat cream cheese
4¼ ounces (120 g)

Eggs
x 2 (yolks)

Feta cheese
1¾ ounces (50 g)

Cooked ham
2 slices

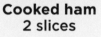

Grated nutmeg
¾ teaspoon

Salt, pepper

Preparation: 10 minutes

• In a salad bowl, mix together the **cream cheese**, **egg** yolks, crushed **feta**, the **ham**, cut into small pieces, and the **nutmeg**.
• Season with salt and pepper.

VINAIGRETTE

20 kcal/person

To serve with:

Salads

Steamed fish, shellfish, or poultry

Steamed or boiled vegetables

White beans

Lentils

Couscous

Orange
x 1

Whole-grain mustard
2 tablespoons (30 g)

Soy sauce
¼ cup (60 mL)

 **Salt, pepper**

👥👥👥👥

🕐

Preparation: 5 minutes

• Squeeze the **orange**. Mix the juice with the **mustard**, **soy sauce**, and 6 tablespoons (90 mL) water. Season with salt and pepper and serve.

CURRY SAUCE

258 kcal/person
___

To serve with:
Steamed poultry or fish
Grilled or steamed seafood
Steamed vegetables
Vegetable sticks
Grilled meat or fish
Baked squash
Whole-grain pasta
Brown rice

Mango
x ½

Apple
x 1

Coconut milk
1⅔ cup (400 mL)

Curry powder
2 tablespoons (12.6 g)

Cilantro
20 leaves

 **Salt, pepper**

👫👫

🕐
**Preparation: 15 minutes
Cooking: 30 minutes**

• Peel the **mango** and **apple** and cut into small pieces. Cook in a casserole with the **coconut milk** and **curry powder** for 30 minutes over very low heat.

• Purée with a hand blender. Season with salt and pepper, add the chopped **cilantro**, and serve.

BARBECUE SAUCE

86 kcal/person

To serve with:

Meat

Fish

Grilled poultry

Grilled or steamed fish or shellfish

Roasts

Skewers of meat or fish

Grilled vegetables

Grilled or steamed sausages

Tofu

Apple
x 1

Red kidney beans
1 can (16 ounces, or 454 g)

Tomato purée
1 tablespoon (16 g)

Soy sauce
6 tablespoons (90 mL)

Honey
3 tablespoons (60 g)

Preparation: 15 minutes
Cooking: 30 minutes

• Peel the **apple** and cut into small pieces. Cook in a casserole with the drained **red kidney beans**, **tomato purée**, **soy sauce**, **honey**, and 1 tablespoon plus 1 teaspoon (20 mL) water for 30 minutes over very low heat. Purée with a hand blender and serve.

TOMATO KETCHUP

61 kcal/person

To serve with:
Whole-grain pasta
Brown rice
Grilled meat, fish, or poultry
Steamed fish and shellfish
Steamed vegetables
Vegetable sticks
Grated fennel
Omelets

Tomatoes
1 pound (445 g)

Tomato purée
1 tablespoon (16 g)

Cider vinegar
2 tablespoons (30 mL)

Sweet onion
x 1

Honey
3 tablespoons (60 g)

 **Salt, pepper**

Preparation: 15 minutes
Cooking: 30 minutes

• Seed and dice the **tomatoes**. Cook in a saucepan for 30 minutes over low heat with the **tomato purée**, **vinegar**, chopped **onion**, **honey**, and 1 tablespoon plus 1 teaspoon (20 mL) water until reduced and thick.

• Purée with a hand blender. Season with salt and pepper and serve.

MUSTARD SAUCE

50 kcal/person

To serve with:
Grilled meat, fish, or poultry
Steamed quenelles
Grilled or poached sausages
Spit-roasted chicken or rabbit
Kidneys
Fried poultry liver
Fried Brussels sprouts
Steamed vegetables
Roasts

Whole-grain mustard
2 tablespoons (30 g)

Mustard
1 tablespoon (15 g)

Low-fat cream cheese
4¼ ounces (120 g)

Dried thyme leaves
2 teaspoons (2 g)

 Salt, pepper

Preparation: 5 minutes
Cooking: 10 minutes

• Mix the ingredients together in a saucepan. Cook for 10 minutes over low heat, stirring continuously. Season with salt and pepper and serve.

BEEF TARTARE WITH EGGPLANT

313 kcal/person

—

Gluten free

—

Lactose free

Basil
1 bunch

Filet of beef
1 pound, 5 ounces (600 g)

Eggplants
x 3 (medium)

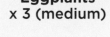

Olive oil
2 tablespoons (30 mL)

 **Salt, pepper**

Preparation: 10 minutes
Cooking: 40 minutes

• Chop the **basil**. Cut the **beef** into small, even cubes.

• Cook the **eggplants** whole for 40 minutes in a steamer and leave to cool. Scoop out the flesh with a spoon and mix with the **beef**, **basil**, and **olive oil**. Season with salt and pepper and serve.

BEEF TARTARE WITH HERBS

229 kcal/person

—

Gluten free

—

Lactose free

Radishes
x 12

Basil
1 bunch

Cilantro
1 bunch

Filet of beef
14 ounces (400 g)

Sesame seeds
2 tablespoons (16 g)

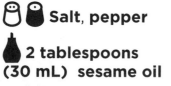

Salt, pepper

2 tablespoons (30 mL) sesame oil

Preparation: 20 minutes

• Trim and dice the **radishes**. Chop the **basil** and **cilantro**.

• Cut the **beef** into small pieces.

• Mix all the ingredients in a salad bowl. Add 2 tablespoons (30 mL) sesame oil, season with salt and pepper, and serve.

STEAMED RIB OF BEEF

586 kcal/person

—

Gluten free

Egg
x 1

Mustard
1 teaspoon (5 g)

Low-fat cream cheese
4¼ ounces (120 g)

Tarragon
1 bunch

Rib of beef
x 1 (not too fatty)

 **Salt**, pepper

👤👤👤👤

🕑
Preparation: 15 minutes
Cooking: 15 minutes

• Separate the **egg**. Beat the yolk with the **mustard**, **cream cheese**, and the chopped **tarragon**.

• Beat the **egg** white until stiff and fold it into the **cream cheese** mixture.

• Cook the **rib of beef** for exactly 15 minutes in a steamer. Cut into slices, season with salt and pepper, and serve with the sauce.

PORK SKEWERS WITH APRICOT

135 kcal/person

—

Lactose free

Pork filet
x 1

Apricots
x 8

Soy sauce
2 tablespoons (30 mL)

Honey
1 tablespoon (20 g)

Cilantro
x 4 sprigs

Preparation: 15 minutes
Cooking: 20 minutes

• Cut the **pork** and **apricots** into evenly sized pieces. Assemble 8 skewers, alternating pieces of meat and fruit.

• Cook the skewers for 20 minutes in a steamer. Arrange in a serving dish and pour the **soy sauce** and **honey** over. Serve with the **cilantro** sprigs.

BLANQUETTE OF VEAL WITH COCONUT MILK

747 kcal/person

—

Gluten free

—

Lactose free

Stewing veal
2½ pounds (1.2 kg)

Coconut milk
1⅔ cups (400 mL)

Snow peas
3½ ounces (100 g)

Peas
3½ ounces (100 g)

Fresh baby spinach
3½ ounces (100 g)

 **Salt, pepper**

**Preparation: 20 minutes
Cooking:
1 hour, 10 minutes**

• Cook the **veal** in a casserole with 1 quart (1 L) water for 1 hour over low heat. Remove the **veal** and set aside. Add the **coconut milk** to the casserole and cook over high heat until reduced by half. Add the **snow peas**, **peas**, and the trimmed **spinach**.

• Cook for 10 minutes more over low heat. Return the meat to the casserole, season and serve.

PORK FILET WITH LEEK

135 kcal/person

—

Lactose free

Leek
x 1

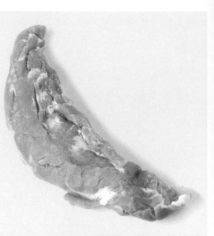
Pork filet
x 1 (without fat)

Whole-grain mustard
3 tablespoons (45 g)

 Salt, pepper

Preparation: 15 minutes
Cooking: 43 minutes

• Cut the **leek** in half lengthwise. Wash under cold running water and plunge it into boiling water for 3 minutes.

• Brush the **pork** with **mustard**, then wrap the **leek** leaves around it. Cook for 40 minutes in a steamer. Season with salt and pepper.

• Cut into thick slices and serve with salad and Mustard Sauce (page 188).

VEAL WITH CARROTS AND ROSEMARY

567 kcal/person

—

Gluten free

—

Lactose free

Stewing veal
2½ pounds (1.2 kg)

Rosemary
3 sprigs

Carrots
x 8

Sweet onions
x 2

 Salt, pepper

👨👨👧👦

🕐
Preparation: 10 minutes
Cooking: 1 hour,
30 minutes

• Place the **veal**, the **rosemary** sprigs, halved, the sliced **carrots**, and the chopped **onion** in a covered casserole.

• Cover with water and cook, covered, for 1 hour, 30 minutes over very low heat. Season with salt and pepper and serve straight from the casserole.

PORK, CHANTERELLES, AND BLUEBERRIES

140 kcal/person

—

Lactose free

Pork filet
x 1 (without fat)

Chanterelles
10½ ounces (300 g)

Blueberries
x 32

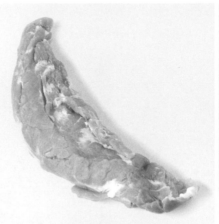

Soy sauce
¼ cup (60 mL)

 **Salt**, pepper

Preparation: 15 minutes
Cooking: 5 minutes

• Cut the **pork** into cubes. Rinse and dry the **chanterelles**.

• Sear the meat for 1 minute in a very hot, dry, nonstick pan. Season with salt and pepper and cook for 1 minute more.

• Add the **chanterelles**, **blueberries**, and **soy sauce**. Cook for 3 minutes more and serve.

CHICKEN WITH PEPPERS AND BASIL

348 kcal/person

—

Gluten free

—

Lactose free

Red bell peppers
x 2

Garlic
6 cloves

White onion
x 1

Chicken breasts
x 4

Basil
1 bunch

 **Salt**, **pepper**

Preparation: 10 minutes
Cooking: 50 minutes

• Cut the **red bell peppers** into pieces. Cook them in a casserole with the peeled **garlic** and chopped **onion** in 6¾ fluid ounces (200 mL) water for 30 minutes over low heat.

• Purée with a hand blender.

• Add the **chicken**, roughly cubed. Season with salt and pepper and cook for 20 minutes more. Remove from the heat, add the **basil**, and serve.

STEAMED FILET STEAK

360 kcal/person

—

Gluten free

Low-fat cream cheese
8½ ounces (240 g)

Whole-grain mustard
¼ cup (60 g)

Raspberry vinegar
2 tablespoons (30 mL)

Dill
2 bunches

Filet steaks
x 4 (6 ounces, or 170 g each)

 **Salt, pepper**

🕐
Preparation: 10 minutes
Cooking: 5 minutes

• Mix together the **cream cheese**, **mustard**, **vinegar**, and three-fourths of the chopped **dill**.
• Season the **steaks** with salt and pepper. Cook for 5 minutes or until desired doneness in a steamer.
• Slice the **steaks** and arrange in a serving dish. Sprinkle with the remaining **dill** and serve with the sauce.

CHICKEN AND WINTER SQUASH SKEWERS

278 kcal/person

—

Gluten free

—

Lactose free

Snow peas
x 32

Winter squash
7 ounces (200 g)

Chicken breasts
1 pound, 5 ounces (600 g)

Balsamic vinegar
2 tablespoons (30 mL)

Sesame seeds
2 tablespoons (16 g)

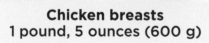 **Salt**, **pepper**

Preparation: 20 minutes
Cooking: 25 minutes

• Preheat the oven to 350°F/180°C.
• Trim the **snow peas**. Cut the **squash** and **chicken** into pieces. Assemble 4 skewers, alternating the **squash**, **chicken**, and **snow peas**.
• Arrange the skewers in an ovenproof dish. Season with salt and pepper, sprinkle with the **vinegar**, and bake for 25 minutes. Sprinkle with **sesame seeds** and serve.

TOMATO BURGER

269 kcal/person

—

Gluten free

—

Lactose free

Hamburgers
x 4 (3½ ounces, or 100 g each)

Tomatoes
x 4 (large)

Mustard
1 teaspoon (5 g)

Cooked ham
2 slices

Lettuce
8 leaves

Salt, pepper

1 drizzle olive oil

Preparation: 15 minutes
Cooking: 7 minutes

• Preheat the oven to 350°F/180°C. Sear the **hamburgers** for 1 minute per side in a pan with a drizzle of olive oil.

• Halve **tomatoes** and brush insides with **mustard**. Place half a slice of **ham** on one **tomato** half, a **hamburger** on the other, and bake 5 minutes.

• Add the **lettuce** leaves and assemble the burgers. Season with salt and pepper and serve.

TURKEY ESCALOPES WITH MUSHROOMS

213 kcal/person

Turkey escalopes
x 4

Soy sauce
¼ cup (60 mL)

Button mushrooms
1.1 pounds (500 g)

Low-fat cream
2 cups (480 mL)

Tarragon
1 bunch

Salt, pepper

1 drizzle olive oil

Preparation: 20 minutes
Cooking: 22 minutes

• Sear the **turkey escalopes** for 1 minute per side in a frying pan with a drizzle of olive oil. Add the **soy sauce**, sliced **mushrooms**, and **cream**.

• Cook for 20 minutes over low heat, stirring continuously. Season with salt and pepper. Add the **tarragon**, mix, and serve.

POACHED CHICKEN WITH GINGER AND LEMONGRASS

477 kcal/person

—

Gluten free

—

Lactose free

Chicken
x 1

Fresh ginger
3½ ounces (100 g)

Lemongrass
4 stalks

White onions
x 2

Thyme
5 sprigs

 **Salt**, pepper

🧍🧍🧍🧍

Preparation: 10 minutes
Cooking: 1 hour

• Place the **chicken** in a casserole with the peeled and sliced **ginger**, **lemongrass**, cut into pieces, thinly sliced **onions**, and **thyme**.
• Cover with water, season with salt and pepper, and simmer for 1 hour over low heat.
• Cut the **chicken** into pieces and serve the bouillon separately.

CHICKEN PARCELS WITH GIROLLES

342 kcal/person

—

Gluten free

Girolles
8½ ounces (240 g)

Fresh goat cheese
5 ounces (150 g)

Chicken breasts
1 pound, 5 ounces (600 g)

Thyme
8 sprigs

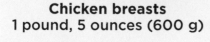 **Salt, pepper**

1 drizzle walnut oil

Preparation: **15 minutes**
Cooking: **25 minutes**

• Wash and dry the **girolles**. Preheat the oven to 350°F/180°C.

• Divide the **cheese**, the **chicken**, cut into pieces, the **girolles**, and the **thyme** among 4 sheets of parchment paper. Close the parcels tightly and bake for 25 minutes.

• Arrange the parcels on plates, season, and serve with a drizzle of walnut oil.

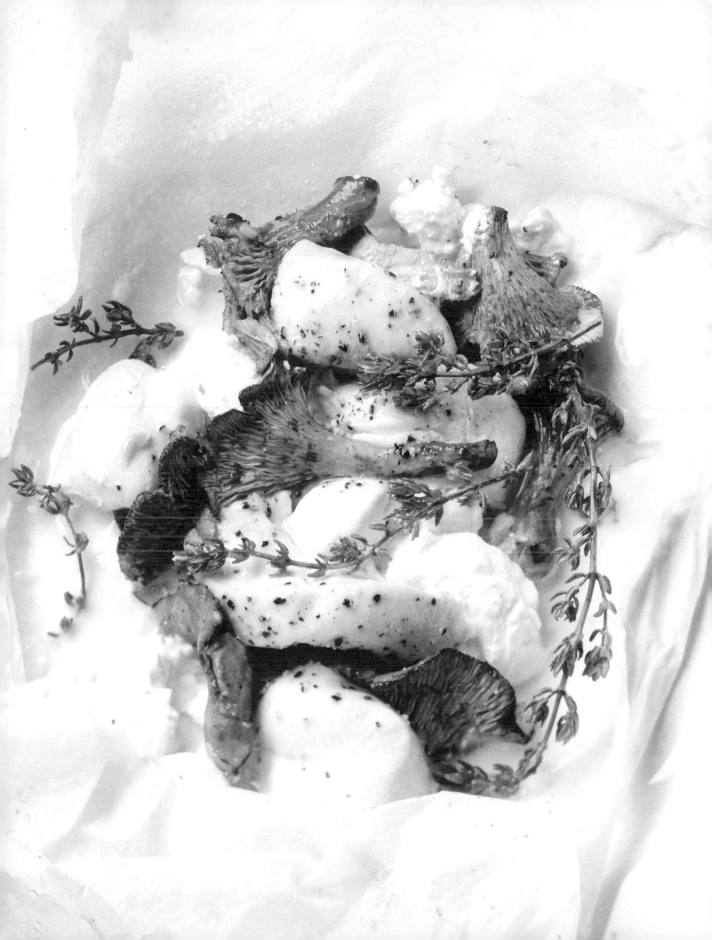

TOMATOES STUFFED WITH BEEF AND EGGPLANT

168 kcal/person

—

Gluten free

—

Lactose free

Eggplants
x 2

Ground beef
7 ounces (200 g)

Dried thyme leaves
2 tablespoons (5 g)

Tomatoes
x 8 (medium)

 **Salt, pepper**

Preparation: 20 minutes
Cooking: 1 hour

• Cook the **eggplants** for 40 minutes in a steamer. Scoop out the flesh and mix with the **beef** and **thyme**. Season with salt and pepper.

• Preheat the oven to 350°F/180°C.

• Hollow out the **tomatoes** and stuff them with the beef and **eggplant** mixture. Arrange in an ovenproof dish, add the scooped out **tomato** flesh to the dish, and bake for 20 minutes. Serve very hot.

PEAS WITH MERGUEZ SAUSAGE AND BROCCOLI

194 kcal/person

—

Gluten free

—

Lactose free

Merguez sausages
x 2

Peas
14 ounces (400 g)

Cherry tomatoes
7 ounces (200 g)

Broccoli
9 ounces (250 g)

Dried oregano
1 tablespoon (3 g)

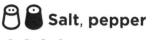 Salt, pepper

Preparation: 15 minutes
Cooking: 42 minutes

• Prick the **sausages** and boil for 20 minutes. Cut into pieces and sear for 1 minute per side in a dry frying pan.

• Add the **peas**, halved **cherry tomatoes**, the **broccoli**, cut into pieces, and the **oregano**. Cook for 20 minutes, stirring frequently. Season with salt and pepper and serve.

LOW-FAT STEW

544 kcal/person

—

Gluten free

—

Lactose free

Chuck steak
2 pounds (900 g)

Turnips
x 4

Carrots
x 4

Fennel
2 bulbs

Bouquet garni
x 1

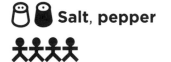 **Salt, pepper**

Preparation: 10 minutes
Cooking: 2 hours

• Place the **steak** in a casserole and just cover with water. Bring to a boil, then pour off the water, and rinse the meat.

• Return the meat to the casserole. Add the peeled **turnips**, **carrots**, **fennel**, the **bouquet garni** and 2 quarts (2 L) water. Cover and cook for 2 hours over low heat. Season with salt and pepper and serve from the casserole.

PANFRIED BEEF WITH CARROTS

299 kcal/person

—

Gluten free

—

Lactose free

Carrots
1 pounds 1½ ounces (500 g)

Steaks
x 4 (1 pound, 5 ounces, or about 600 g)

Flat-leaf parsley
4 sprigs

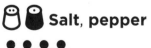

Olive oil
2 tablespoons (30 mL)

Salt, pepper

Preparation: 20 minutes
Cooking: 5 minutes

• Peel and grate the **carrots**. Cut the **steaks** into small pieces. Chop the **parsley**.

• Heat the **olive oil** in a frying pan and sear the meat. Fry for 3 minutes over high heat. Add the **carrots** and **parsley**. Season with salt and pepper, cook for 2 minutes more, or until your desired doneness, stirring continuously, and serve.

TURKEY ESCALOPES WITH TOMATO

202 kcal/person

—

Gluten free

—

Lactose free

Turkey escalopes
x 4 (fairly thin)

Tomatoes
x 3 (large)

White wine
3 fluid ounces (80 mL)

Bouquets garnis
x 2

 Salt, **pepper**

Preparation: 10 minutes
Cooking: 45 minutes

• Preheat the oven to 350°F/180°C. Cut the **turkey escalopes** in half.
• Cut the **tomatoes** into thick slices and arrange them in a gratin dish, interspersed with the meat.
• Add the **white wine** and **bouquets garnis**. Season with salt and pepper. Bake for 45 minutes, basting occasionally.

TURKEY, WINTER SQUASH, AND SAGE PARCELS

265 kcal/person

—

Gluten free

—

Lactose free

Winter squash
14 ounces (400 g)

Turkey escalopes
x 4

Paprika
1 tablespoon (7 g)

Sage
12 leaves

Walnut oil
2 tablespoons (30 mL)

 **Salt, pepper**

👤👤👤👤

🕐
Preparation: 15 minutes
Cooking: 35 minutes

• Preheat the oven to 350°F/180°C. Peel and cut the **squash** and the **turkey escalopes** into same-size pieces.

• Divide the **squash** and **turkey** pieces with the **paprika** and **sage** among 4 sheets of parchment paper. Season with salt and pepper and close the parcels tightly. Bake for 35 minutes. Transfer to plates and serve with the **walnut oil** drizzled over.

RABBIT IN WHITE WINE SAUCE WITH MUSHROOMS

407 kcal/person

—

Gluten free

—

Lactose free

Rabbit legs
x 4

Button mushrooms
1 pound (445 g)

Carrots
x 4 (large)

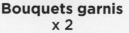
Bouquets garnis
x 2

White wine
17 fluid ounces (500 mL)

Salt, pepper

**Preparation: 15 minutes
Cooking: 1 hour,
30 minutes**

• Place the **rabbit legs**, the **mushrooms**, cut into quarters, the peeled and sliced **carrots**, and the **bouquets garnis** in a casserole.

• Add the **white wine** and 1¼ cups (300 mL) water. Cover and simmer for 1 hour, 30 minutes over very low heat. Season with salt and pepper and serve straight from the casserole.

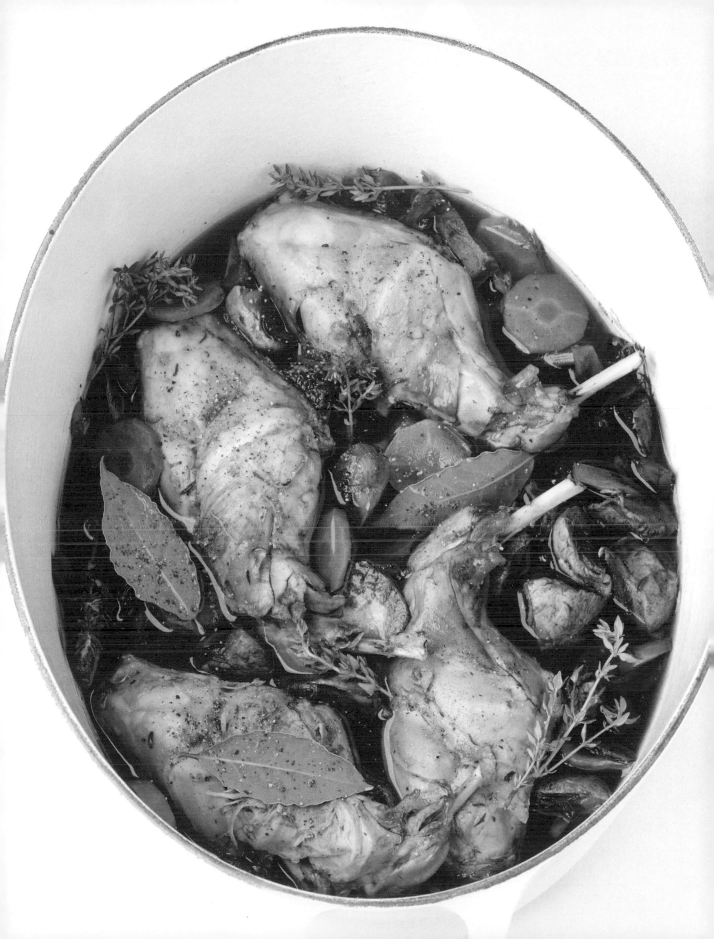

STUFFED EGGPLANT

140 kcal/person

—

Gluten free

Eggplants
x 2

Ground beef
7 ounces (200 g)

Sour cream
¼ cup (60 g)

Cumin seeds
2 teaspoons (4 g)

Cilantro
12 sprigs

Salt, pepper

Preparation: 20 minutes
Cooking: 1 hour

• Cook the **eggplants** whole for 40 minutes in a steamer. Scoop out the flesh with a spoon and mix with the **beef**, **sour cream**, **cumin**, and chopped **cilantro**. Season with salt and pepper.

• Preheat the oven to 350°F/180°C.

• Stuff the **eggplants** with the meat mixture and bake for 20 minutes, or until your desired doneness. Serve hot.

LAMB STEW

581 kcal/person

—

Gluten free

—

Lactose free

Lamb leg, chump off
x 1 (2½ pounds, or about 1.2 kg)

Bouquets garnis
x 2

Leek
x 1

Baby turnips
1 bunch

Baby carrots
1 bunch

Salt, pepper

Preparation: 20 minutes
Cooking: 2 hours

• Remove the fat from the **lamb** and cook for 1 hour in a large casserole with the **bouquets garnis** in 3 quarts (3 L) of water.

• Add the washed and chopped **leek**, the peeled **turnips**, and **carrots**, and cook for 1 hour more over low heat. Season with salt and pepper and serve straight from the casserole.

STEAMED MEATBALLS WITH BASIL

321 kcal/person

—

Lactose free

Basil
1 bunch

Ground beef
1 pound (445 g)

Cumin seeds
1 tablespoon (6 g)

Aniseed
1 tablespoon (6.7 g)

 **Salt, pepper**

1 drizzle olive oil

Preparation: 20 minutes
Cooking: 3 minutes

• Chop the **basil**. Mix the **beef** with the spices and **basil**. Season with salt and pepper.

• Shape into 8 same-size meatballs and cook in a steamer for 3 minutes, or until your desired doneness.

• Serve the meatballs with a drizzle of olive oil.

QUINOA WITH CHICKEN

530 kcal/person

—

Gluten free

Chicken legs
x 4

Merguez sausages
x 2

Zucchini
x 2

Carrots
x 4

Quinoa
9 ounces (250 g)

Salt, pepper

Preparation: 15 minutes
Cooking: 35 minutes

• Remove skin from the **chicken legs**. Cook for 35 minutes in a steamer with the **sausages**, the **zucchini**, cut into thick rounds, and peeled **carrots**.
• Cook the **quinoa** in 1 quart (1 L) of water according to package directions. Spread in a serving dish and add the meat and vegetables. Season with salt and pepper and serve with fresh cilantro or cumin seeds, if desired.

STEAMED FILET STEAK WITH TARRAGON

332 kcal/person

—

Gluten free

Tarragon
2 bunches

Low-fat cream cheese
3 ounces (80 g)

Steaks
x 4 (6 ounces, or 170 g each)

 **Salt**, **pepper**

Preparation: 5 minutes
Cooking: 5 minutes

• Mix half the chopped **tarragon** with the **cream cheese**.

• Ten minutes before serving, cook the **steaks** for 5 minutes, or to your desired doneness, in a steamer. Let rest for 30 seconds.

• Spread the **tarragon** mixture over the base of a serving dish and arrange the sliced meat on top. Sprinkle with the remaining **tarragon** and season.

ROAST CHICKEN LEGS WITH MUSTARD

294 kcal/person

—

Gluten free

Low-fat cream cheese
6 ounces (180 g)

Mustard
¼ cup (60 g)

Thyme
4 sprigs

Chicken legs
x 4

Salt, pepper

Preparation: 10 minutes
Cooking: 40 minutes

• Preheat the oven to 350°F/180°C. Mix the **cream cheese** with the **mustard** and **thyme**. Season with salt and pepper.
• Remove the skin from the **chicken legs**. Brush the **chicken** with the **mustard** mixture. Place in an ovenproof dish, bake for 40 minutes, and serve.

SALMON, AVOCADO, AND MUSHROOMS

477 kcal/person

—

Gluten free

—

Lactose free

Salmon steaks
x 4 (with skin)

Avocado
x 1

Chives
1 bunch

Button mushrooms
x 8 (large)

Lime
x 1

 **Salt**, **pepper**

👪👪

🕐

Preparation: 15 minutes
Cooking: 20 minutes

• Preheat the oven to 350°F/180°C. Cook the **salmon steaks**, skin-side down, for 20 minutes.
• Peel and slice the **avocado**. Chop the **chives** and slice the **mushrooms** thinly. Mix with the juice of the **lime**. Serve the **salmon** hot, covered with the **avocado** and **mushroom** mixture, and season with salt and pepper.

POACHED SCALLOPS WITH SAFFRON

58 kcal/person

—

Gluten free

—

Lactose free

Green asparagus
x 8

Cherry tomatoes
x 8

Saffron
5 threads

Scallops
x 12 (with or without coral)

 **Salt**, pepper

⏱
Preparation: 15 minutes
Cooking: 5 minutes

• Trim the **asparagus** and cut it into pieces. Halve the **tomatoes**.

• Place all ingredients in a casserole with 17 fluid ounces (500 mL) water and cook for 5 minutes over very low heat. Season with salt and pepper, let stand for 5 minutes, and serve.

BAKED BASS WITH A VITAMIN-RICH SAUCE

273 kcal/person

—

Lactose free

Kiwi
x 2

Passion fruit
x 2

Soy sauce
¼ cup (60 mL)

Cilantro
1 bunch

Whole bass
x 1 (2 pounds, or 900 g),
scaled and gutted

Salt, pepper

Preparation: 10 minutes
Cooking: 25 minutes

• Preheat the oven to 350°F/180°C. Peel and dice the **kiwi**. Scoop out the pulp of the **passion fruit** and mix with the **kiwi**, **soy sauce**, and chopped **cilantro**.

• Bake the **bass** whole for 25 minutes. Prick to test if it is cooked. Season with salt and pepper and serve with the sauce. Garnish with lemon slices and thyme sprigs, if desired.

COD WITH HERBS

168 kcal/person

—

Lactose free

Mandarins
x 3

Cod loin
1¼ pounds (800 g)

Soy sauce
¼ cup (60 mL)

Basil
1 bunch

Cilantro
1 bunch

1 drizzle olive oil

Preparation: 15 minutes
Cooking: 10 minutes

• Preheat the oven to 350°F/180°C. Roughly chop the herbs. Squeeze the **mandarins** and strain the juice.

• Put the **cod** in an ovenproof dish and bake for 10 minutes. Pour the **mandarin** juice and **soy sauce** over. Sprinkle with the herbs and serve with a drizzle of olive oil.

CHINESE-STYLE SEA BREAM

210 kcal/person

—

Lactose free

Fresh ginger
5 ounces (150 g)

Leek
x 1 (small)

Lemon grass
2 stems

Red sea bream
x 1, (2 pounds, or 900 g)
scaled and gutted

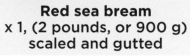
Soy sauce
¼ cup (60 mL)

Preparation: 20 minutes
Cooking: 30 minutes

• Preheat the oven to 350°F/180°C. Peel the **ginger** and grate with a hand grater. Wash and cut the **leek** and the **lemongrass** into very thin strips.
• Place the **sea bream** in an ovenproof dish. Add the other ingredients and a glass of water, then bake in the oven for 30 minutes, basting regularly with the cooking juices. Serve with the **soy sauce** drizzled over. Garnish with cilantro leaves, if desired.

OCTOPUS WITH HERBS

180 kcal/person

—

Gluten free

—

Lactose free

Octopus
x 1 (2 pounds, or about 1 kg)

Cherry tomatoes
1.5 pounds (650 g)

White wine
3 tablespoons plus
1 teaspoon (50 mL)

Capers
3½ ounces (100 g)

Bouquet garni
x 1

 **Salt, pepper**

Preparation: 15 minutes
Cooking: 40 minutes

• Place the **octopus** in a casserole. Cover with water and bring to a boil. Cook for 20 minutes, remove from the heat, and let **octopus** cool in the casserole.

• Cook the halved **tomatoes** for 20 minutes with the **white wine**, 3 tablespoons plus 1 teaspoon (50 mL) of the cooking water, the **capers**, and the **bouquet garni**. Add the **octopus**, cut into pieces. Season with salt and pepper and serve.

SAUERKRAUT WITH SHRIMP AND CUMIN

365 kcal/person

—

Lactose free

Cooked sauerkraut
1 pound (445 g)

Beer
6 ¾ fluid ounces (200 mL)

Cumin seeds
2 tablespoons (12 g)

Raw giant shrimp
x 4 (peeled)

Dill
1 bunch

 **Salt, pepper**

Preparation: 5 minutes
Cooking: 20 minutes

• In a casserole, cook the **sauerkraut** with the **beer** and **cumin** for 20 minutes over low heat. After 10 minutes, add the halved **shrimp**. Season with salt and pepper.

• Transfer the **shrimp sauerkraut** to a serving dish, sprinkle with chopped **dill**, and serve.

MACKEREL PARCELS

240 kcal/person

—

Gluten free

—

Lactose free

Leek
x 1 (small)

Mackerel
4 fillets

Rosemary
4 sprigs

Whole-grain mustard
2 tablespoons (30 g)

Preparation: 15 minutes
Cooking: 20 minutes

• Preheat the oven to 350°F/180°C. Divide the washed and thinly sliced **leek**, **mackerel**, **rosemary**, and **mustard** among 4 sheets of parchment paper.
• Close the parcels tightly and bake for 20 minutes. Transfer to plates and serve.

CLAMS MARINIÈRE WITH HAM

270 kcal/person

—

Gluten free

Cooked ham
3 slices (without rind)

Clams
x 60 (cleaned)

Lemon thyme
1 bunch

Low-fat cream
6 ¾ fluid ounces (200 mL)

Preparation: 20 minutes
Cooking: 10 minutes

• Chop the **ham** very finely. Cook the **clams** over high heat in 1 tablespoon plus 1 teaspoon (20 mL) water with the **thyme** until they open. Discard any clams that do not open.

• Divide the **clams** among 4 bowls. Strain the cooking liquid, add the **cream** to it, and bring to a boil. Pour the **cream** mixture over the **clams**.

• Add the chopped **ham**, mix gently, and serve.

STEAMED SWORDFISH WITH HERBS

237 kcal/person

—

Gluten free

Cherry tomatoes
x 8

Capers
4 teaspoons (12 g)

Dried oregano
2 teaspoons (2 g)

Olive oil
2 tablespoons (30 mL)

Swordfish
4 pieces

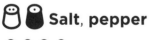 **Salt, pepper**

Preparation: 10 minutes
Cooking: 5 minutes

• Cut the **tomatoes** into quarters and mix with the **capers**, **oregano**, and **olive oil**. Season with salt and pepper.

• Cook the **swordfish** for 5 minutes in a steamer. Transfer to a serving dish, pour the **tomato** and herb mixture over, and serve.

POLLOCK PARCELS WITH LEMON

150 kcal/person

—

Gluten free

—

Lactose free

Pollock
4 fillets

Tomatoes
x 4 (medium)

Lemons
x 2

Rosemary
4 sprigs

Black olives
x 20 (pitted)

 **Salt, pepper**

👤👤👤👤

🕐
Preparation: 10 minutes
Cooking: 15 minutes

• Preheat the oven to 350°F/180°C.
• Divide the **pollock**, sliced **tomatoes** and **lemons**, **rosemary**, and **olives** among 4 sheets of parchment paper.
• Close the parcels tightly. Bake for 15 minutes. Transfer to plates, season with salt and pepper, and serve.

COD WITH MUSHROOMS

170 kcal/person

—

Lactose free

Cod
4 fillets

Chanterelles
7 ounces (200 g)

Girolles
7 ounces (200 g)

Soy sauce
½ cup (120 mL)

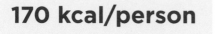
Tarragon
1 bunch

Preparation: 10 minutes
Cooking: 15 minutes

• Preheat the oven to 350°F/180°C. Place the **cod** in a large ovenproof dish, add the washed and chopped **mushrooms**, 1 tablespoon plus 1 teaspoon (20 mL) water, and the **soy sauce**. Bake for 15 minutes.

• Add the **tarragon** and serve straight from the ovenproof dish.

SALMON PAUPIETTES

410 kcal/person

—

Steam

—

Gluten free

Salmon fillets
14 ounces (400 g), skinless

Salmon roe
4 teaspoons (21 g)

Limes
x 2

Smoked salmon
8 slices

Salt, pepper

Preparation: 15 minutes
Cooking: 3 minutes

• Cut the **salmon** into pieces and mix with the **roe** and the **lime juice**. Season with salt and pepper.
• Arrange the mixture in the middle of the slices of **smoked salmon**. Roll up carefully to form small paupiettes.
• Place the paupiettes on parchment paper and cook for 3 minutes in a steamer. Serve garnished with any additional roe.

COD PARCELS

120 kcal/person

—

Gluten free

—

Lactose free

Cucumber
3½ ounces (100 g)

Cod loin steaks
1 pound, 5 ounces (600 g)

Radishes
x 12

Aniseed
2 teaspoons (4.5 g)

 **Salt, pepper**

1 drizzle olive oil

Preparation: 15 minutes
Cooking: 25 minutes

- Preheat the oven to 350°F/180°C.
- Divide the thinly sliced **cucumber** among 4 sheets of parchment paper. Add the **cod loin steaks** and thinly sliced **radishes**. Sprinkle with **aniseed** and season with salt and pepper.
- Close the parcels tightly and bake for 25 minutes. Serve with a drizzle of olive oil.

SEA BREAM PARCELS WITH THYME

133 kcal/person

—

Gluten free

—

Lactose free

Sea bream
4 fillets

Cherry tomatoes
x 12

Zucchini
x 2 (small)

Thyme
12 sprigs

Bay leaves
x 4

 Salt, pepper

1 drizzle olive oil

♛♛♛♛

Preparation: 20 minutes
Cooking: 25 minutes

• Preheat the oven to 350°F/180°C.
• Divide the **sea bream** among 4 sheets of parchment paper. Add the halved **tomatoes**, grated **zucchini**, **thyme**, and **bay leaves**. Season with salt and pepper.
• Close the parcels tightly and bake for 25 minutes. Serve with a drizzle of olive oil.

SALMON WITH ASPARAGUS

104 kcal/person

—

Gluten free

—

Lactose free

Green asparagus
x 16

Salmon steaks
x 4

Pumpkin seeds
2 tablespoons (8 g)

 **Salt, pepper**

1 drizzle olive oil

Preparation: 10 minutes
Cooking: 5 minutes

• Trim the **asparagus** and cut into pieces.
• Place the **salmon steaks**, **asparagus** pieces, and **pumpkin seeds** in a steamer. Season with salt and pepper and cook for 5 minutes.
• Transfer the **salmon steaks** to plates. Add a drizzle of olive oil and serve.

SCALLOP AND SHRIMP PARCELS

135 kcal/person

—

Gluten free

—

Lactose free

Scallops
x 12

Raw shrimp
x 12 (peeled)

Grape tomatoes
x 24, red and yellow

White wine
¼ cup (60 mL)

Dried oregano
1 tablespoon (3 g)

Salt, pepper

1 drizzle olive oil

Preparation: 10 minutes
Cooking: 25 minutes

• Preheat the oven to 350°F/180°C.
• Divide the **scallops** and **shrimp** among 4 sheets of parchment paper. Add the **tomatoes**, **white wine**, and **oregano**. Season with salt and pepper.
• Close the parcels tightly and bake for 25 minutes. Serve with a drizzle of olive oil.

MULLET WITH ORANGE AND ROSEMARY

200 kcal/person

—

Gluten free

—

Lactose free

Whole mullet
x 4 (scaled and gutted)

Rosemary
2 sprigs

Garlic
4 cloves

Orange
x 1

Limes
x 2

Salt, pepper

1 drizzle olive oil

Preparation: 15 minutes
Cooking: 15 minutes
Marinating: 2 hours

• Place the **mullet** in a large ovenproof dish. Add the **rosemary**, chopped **garlic**, and the juice of the **orange** and **limes**. Season with salt and pepper and marinate for 2 hours in the refrigerator.

• Preheat the oven to 350°F/180°C. Bake the **mullet** in the marinade for 15 minutes. Serve with a drizzle of olive oil and any additional rosemary sprigs.

SCALLOPS WITH CREAMED PARSNIPS

140 kcal/person

—

Gluten free

—

Lactose free

Parsnips
10½ ounces (300 g)

Scallops
x 8 + 4 clean shells

Thyme
4 sprigs

Organic lemons
x 3

🧂🧂 **Salt, pepper**

🫗 **1 drizzle olive oil**

👫👫

🕐

Preparation: 20 minutes
Cooking: 35 minutes

• Cook the **parsnips** for 30 minutes in a saucepan with just enough water to cover. Purée with a hand blender.

• Preheat the oven to 350°F/180°C. Season the parsnips and spoon the purée into 4 **scallop shells**. Add the raw **scallops** and **thyme**. Grate the zest of the **lemons** over the **scallops**. Bake for 5 minutes and serve with a drizzle of olive oil.

OCTOPUS CURRY

594 kcal/person

—

Gluten free

—

Lactose free

Basil
1 bunch

Zucchini
x 2

Coconut milk
27 fluid ounces (800 mL)

Curry powder
2 tablespoons (30 g)

Octopus
x 1 (about 2 pounds, or 1 kg)

Preparation: 25 minutes
Cooking: 45 minutes

• Chop the **basil**. Slice the **zucchini** and cook in the **coconut milk** with the **curry powder** for 25 minutes over low heat.

• Place the **octopus** in a casserole, cover with water, and bring to the boil. Cook for 20 minutes, then take off the heat and leave to cool in the casserole.

• Cut the **octopus** into pieces and add to the **zucchini** mixture with the **basil**. Reheat and serve.

MULLET, CELERIAC, AND APPLE

224 kcal/person

—

Gluten free

—

Lactose free

Apple
x 1

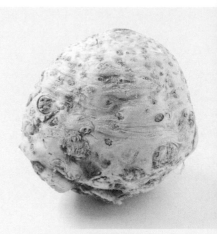

Celeriac
1 pound, 5 ounces (600 g)

Mullet
8 fillets

Fennel seeds
1 tablespoon (5.8 g)

Salt, **pepper**

1 drizzle olive oil

Preparation: 20 minutes
Cooking: 45 minutes

• Cut the **apple** (reserving a few slices) and peeled **celeriac** into cubes. Cook in a saucepan in 17 fluid ounces (500 mL) water for 35 minutes over low heat. Purée with a hand blender and season.

• Preheat oven to 350°F/180°C. Pour the purée into a gratin dish. Arrange **mullet** and reserved **apple** slices on top. Sprinkle with **fennel seeds** and bake for 10 minutes. Serve with a drizzle of olive oil.

FILLET OF BASS WITH TOMATO

134 kcal/person

—

Gluten free

Bass
4 fillets (skinless)

Tomatoes
x 4 (medium)

Basil
12 large leaves

 **Salt, pepper**

1 drizzle olive oil

Preparation: 15 minutes
Cooking: 10 minutes

• Cut the **bass** in thirds and the **tomatoes** in fourths. Insert a piece of **bass** and a **basil** leaf between each layer of **tomato**. Season with salt and pepper. Secure each **tomato** together with a cocktail pick and cook for 10 minutes in a steamer.

• Transfer the **tomatoes** to plates, remove the cocktail picks, and serve with a drizzle of olive oil.

SCALLOPS WITH HONEY AND ASPARAGUS

64 kcal/person

—

Lactose free

Green asparagus
x 12

Honey
2 tablespoons (40 g)

Scallops
x 12

Thyme
4 sprigs

Soy sauce
3 tablespoons (45 mL)

Salt, **pepper**

Preparation: 10 minutes
Cooking: 9 minutes

• Trim the **asparagus** and cut into pieces.
• Heat the **honey** in a frying pan. Sear the **scallops** and **asparagus** for 3 minutes per side in the foaming **honey**. Add the **thyme** and **soy sauce**.
• Cook for 3 minutes, stirring continuously, season with salt and pepper, and serve.

THAI-STYLE SPICED SCALLOPS

130 kcal/person

—

Gluten free

—

Lactose free

Scallops
x 16 (with or without coral)

Fresh ginger
1¾ ounces (50 g)

Lemongrass
2 stalks

Red chile
x 1 (optional)

Basil
20 leaves

Preparation: 10 minutes
Cooking: 15 minutes

• Preheat the oven to 350°F/180°C. Divde the **scallops**, the peeled and grated **ginger**, the **lemongrass**, and the finely chopped **chile**, if using, among 4 sheets of parchment paper.
• Close the parcels tightly and bake for 15 minutes. Add the **basil** leaves and serve.

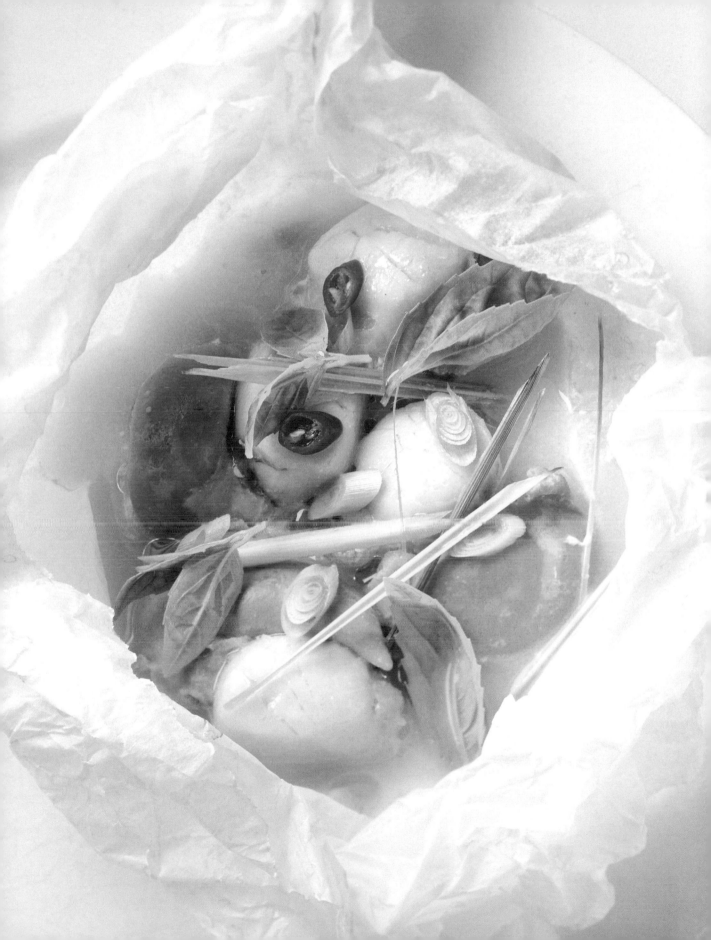

ASIAN-STYLE COD LOIN

367 kcal/person

—

Gluten free

—

Lactose free

Red bell peppers
x 2

Coconut milk
1⅔ cups (400 mL)

Cod loin steaks
x 4 (6 ounces, or about
180 g each)

Preserved lemons
x 2

Black olives
x 20 (pitted)

Salt, pepper

1 drizzle olive oil

Preparation: 25 minutes
Cooking: 40 minutes

• Cut the **peppers** into pieces and cook for 20 minutes in the **coconut milk** over medium heat. Purée with a hand blender. Season with salt and pepper.

• Preheat the oven to 350°F/180°C. Place the **cod** in an ovenproof dish and cover with the **pepper** coulis. Add the **preserved lemons**, cut into pieces, and the **olives**. Bake for 20 minutes. Serve with a drizzle of olive oil.

MONKFISH CHEEKS WITH TOMATO

195 kcal/person

—

Gluten free

—

Lactose free

Monkfish cheeks
1 pound, 5 ounces (600 g)

Cherry tomatoes
1 pound (445 g)

White wine
about 7 tablespooons
(100 mL)

Olive oil
1 tablespoon (15 mL)

Basil
20 leaves

Salt, pepper

Preparation: 10 minutes
Cooking: 25 minutes

• In a casserole, cook the **monkfish cheeks** for 25 minutes over low heat with the halved **tomatoes**, **white wine**, 1 tablespoon plus 1 teaspoon (20 mL) water, and the **olive oil**.
• Season with salt and pepper. Add the **basil** leaves, mix, and serve.

STEWED MONKFISH WITH SAFFRON

193 kcal/person

—

Gluten free

—

Lactose free

Monkfish
x 1 (1¾ pounds, or about 800 g)

Carrots
x 4

Leek
x 1

Turnips
x 6

Saffron
10 threads

 **Salt, pepper**

👤👤👤👤

🕐
Preparation: 15 minutes
Cooking: 45 minutes

• In a casserole, cook the **monkfish**, trussed if desired, peeled **carrots**, washed and halved **leek**, peeled and chopped **turnips**, and **saffron** in 1½ quarts (1.5 L) water for 45 minutes over very low heat. Add a little water if the bouillon reduces too much. Season with salt and pepper. Serve straight from the casserole.

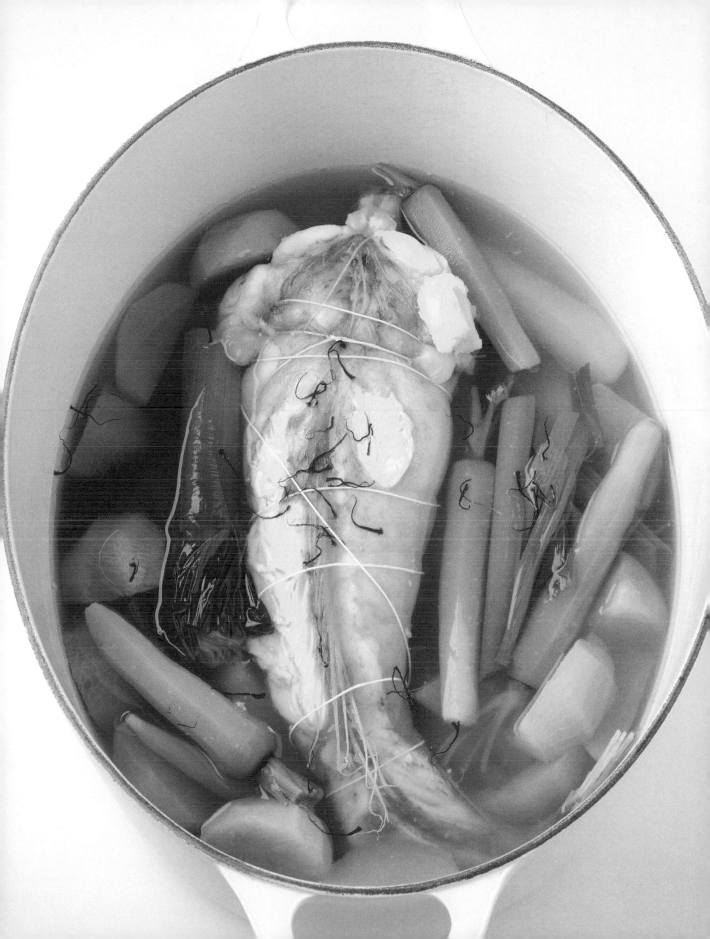

SALMON PARCELS WITH VEGETABLES

322 kcal/person

—

Gluten free

—

Lactose free

Salmon steaks
x 4 (5 ounces, or 150 g each)

Zucchini
x 1

Peas
7 ounces (200 g)

Snow peas
4 ounces (120 g)

Basil
1 bunch

 **Salt, pepper**

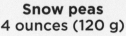 **1 drizzle olive oil**

- Preheat the oven to 350°F/180°C.
- Divide the **salmon steaks**, **zucchini** cut into rounds, **peas**, and **snow peas** among 4 sheets of parchment paper. Close the parcels tightly.
- Bake for 15 minutes. Sprinkle with the **basil**, season with salt and pepper, and serve with a drizzle of olive oil.

Preparation: 15 minutes
Cooking: 15 minutes

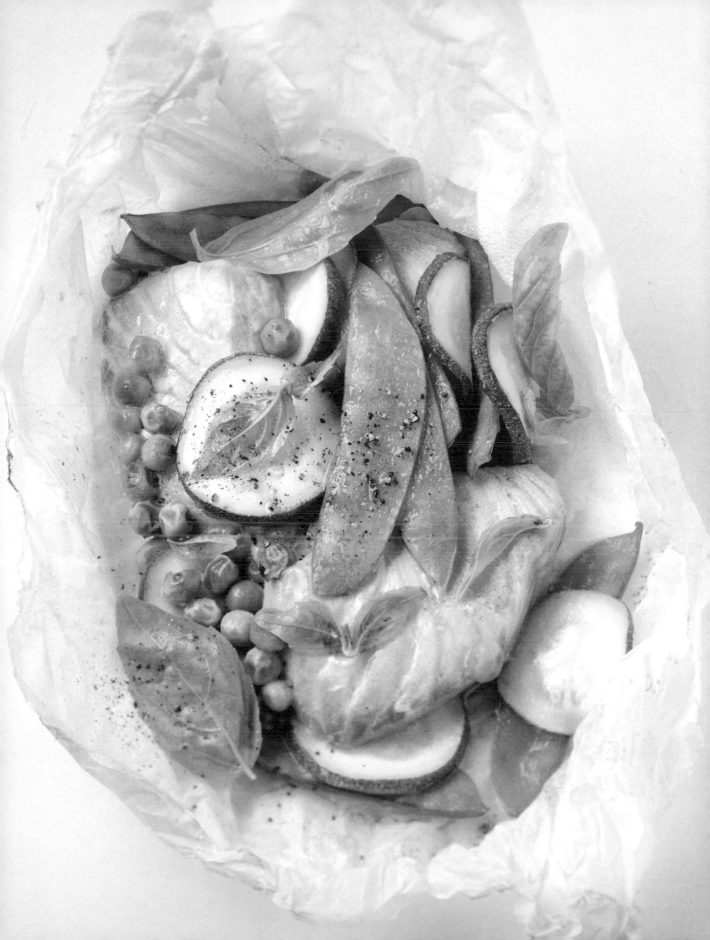

WHITING AND SHELLFISH PARCELS

178 kcal/person

—

Gluten free

—

Lactose free

Whiting
4 fillets

Raw shrimp
x 8 (peeled)

Cockles
x 20 (cleaned)

Mussels
x 20 (cleaned and debearded)

Thyme
8 sprigs

Preparation: 15 minutes
Cooking: 20 minutes

• Preheat the oven to 350°F/180°C.
• Divde the **whiting**, **shrimp**, **cockles**, **mussels**, and **thyme** among 4 sheets of parchment paper. Close the parcels tightly.
• Bake for 20 minutes. Discard any unopened shellfish. Transfer to plates and serve.

JAPANESE-STYLE MACKEREL

304 kcal/person

—

Lactose free

Mackerel
4 fillets (5 ounces, or 150 g each)

Radishes
x 16

Pickled ginger
1 ounce (30 g)

Soy sauce
1 tablespoon (15 mL)

Wasabi
1 teaspoon

Preparation: 15 minutes
Cooking: 20 minutes

• Preheat the oven to 350°F/180°C.
• Divide the **mackerel**, **radishes**, cut into rounds, **ginger**, **soy sauce**, and **wasabi** among 4 sheets of parchment paper. Close the parcels tightly.
• Bake for 20 minutes. Transfer to plates and serve.

MUSSEL PARCELS WITH ROSEMARY

180 kcal/person

—

Gluten free

—

Lactose free

Mussels
2 quarts (2 L), cleaned and debearded

Rosemary
8 sprigs

Cherry tomatoes
x 20

Salt, pepper

Preparation: 10 minutes
Cooking: 20 minutes

• Preheat the oven to 350°F/180°C. Divide the **mussels**, **rosemary**, and the halved **tomatoes** among 4 sheets of parchment paper. Close the parcels tightly.
• Bake for 20 minutes. Discard any unopened mussels. Season with salt and pepper, transfer to plates, and serve.

PEA, GOAT CHEESE, AND SPINACH QUICHE

264 kcal/person

—

Vegetarian

—

Gluten free

Fresh goat cheese
10½ ounces or (300 g)

Peas
14 ounces (400 g)

Fresh baby spinach
5 ounces (150 g)

Tarragon
1 bunch

Eggs
x 4

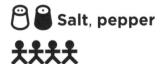 **Salt, pepper**

♟♟♟♟

🕐
Preparation: 30 minutes
Cooking: 25 minutes

• Preheat the oven to 400°F/200°C. Cover the base of a large tart pan with moistened parchment paper.

• Mix together the **goat cheese**, **peas**, trimmed **spinach**, chopped **tarragon**, and **eggs**. Season with salt and pepper.

• Pour the mixture into the prepared pan, pressing it down. Bake for 25 minutes. Serve hot or cold.

STUFFED ZUCCHINI BLOSSOMS

273 kcal/person

—

Vegetarian

—

Gluten free

Ricotta cheese
14 ounces (400 g)

Dried oregano
2 teaspoons (2 g)

Egg
x 1

Organic lemons
x 2

Zucchini blossoms
x 8

 **Salt, pepper**

1 drizzle olive oil

Preparation: 20 minutes
Cooking: 25 minutes

• Preheat the oven to 350°F/180°C. Mix together the **ricotta**, **oregano**, **egg**, and the juice and grated zest of the **lemons**. Season with salt and pepper.
• Using a small spoon, carefully fill the blossoms with the cheese mixture. Place the **zucchini blossoms** in an ovenproof dish and bake for 25 minutes. Serve warm or cold with a drizzle of olive oil.

VEGETABLE COUSCOUS

97 kcal/person

—

Vegetarian

—

Lactose free

Cilantro
1 bunch

Baby carrots
1 bunch

Baby turnips
1 bunch

Radishes
x 12

Cauliflower
2 pounds (900 g)

**1 drizzle olive oil**

♂♂♂♂

🕐
Preparation: 25 minutes
Cooking: 20 minutes

- Chop the **cilantro**.
- Peel the **carrots** and **turnips** and trim the **radishes**. Remove the **cauliflower** stalks and leaves and grate the rest. Spread on a sheet of parchment paper and place the other vegetables on top. Cook for 20 minutes in a steamer.
- Serve with the **cilantro** and a drizzle of olive oil.

TOMATO, GOAT CHEESE, AND ROSEMARY TART

225 kcal/person

—

Vegetarian

—

Gluten free

Fresh goat cheese
10½ ounces (300 g)

Yellow cherry tomatoes
10½ ounces (300 g)

Rosemary
1 sprig

Eggs
x 4

 Salt, **pepper**

**Preparation: 30 minutes
Cooking: 25 minutes**

• Preheat the oven to 400°F/200°C. Cover the base of a large tart pan with moistened parchment paper.

• Mix together the **goat cheese**, **tomatoes**, cut into pieces, chopped **rosemary**, and **eggs**. Season with salt and pepper.

• Pour the mixture into the prepared pan, pressing it down. Bake for 25 minutes. Serve hot or cold.

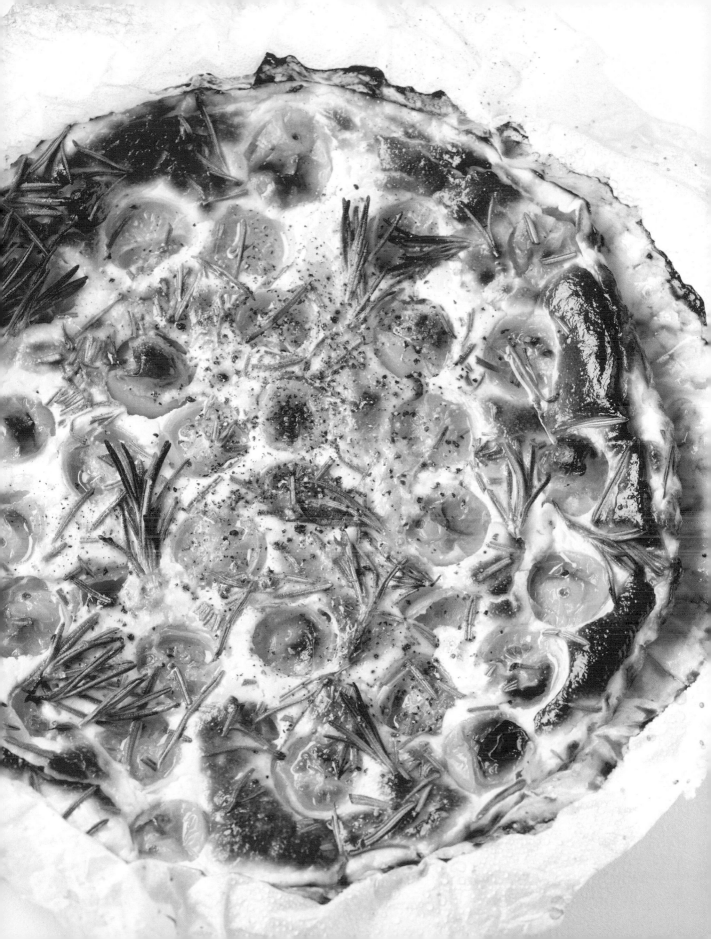

VEGETABLE STEW

31 kcal/person

—

Vegetarian

Leek
x 1

Carrots
x 4

Golden ball turnips
x 4

Sage
1 bunch

 Salt, pepper

👤👤👤👤

🕐

Preparation: 20 minutes
Cooking: 1 hour

• Wash the **leek** and cut it into thirds lengthwise. Peel the **carrots** and **turnips**.

• In a casserole, cook the vegetables with the **sage** in 2 quarts (2 L) of water for 1 hour over very low heat. Season with salt and pepper and serve.

GREEN VEGETABLES IN A RED PEPPER COULIS

117 kcal/person

—

Vegetarian

Snow peas
14 ounces (400 g)

Peas
7 ounces (200 g)

Broccoli
7 ounces (200 g)

Red bell peppers
x 2

Oregano
2 teaspoons (2 g)

 Salt, pepper

Preparation: 10 minutes
Cooking: 25 minutes

• Cook the **snow peas**, **peas**, and **broccoli**, cut into pieces, for 10 minutes in a steamer.
• In a saucepan, cook the **peppers** in about 7 tablespoons (100 mL) water for 15 minutes. Season with salt and pepper and purée with a hand blender.
• Pour the **red pepper** coulis into a serving dish. Top with the vegetables and sprinkle with the **oregano**.

318

CLEMENTINE AND PISTACHIO SALAD

118 kcal/person

—

Gluten free

—

Lactose free

Blanched pistachios
2 tablespoons (16 g)

Honey
1 tablespoon (20 g)

Orange flower water
¼ cup (60 mL)

Clementines
x 16

Tarragon
4 sprigs

𝄞𝄞𝄞𝄞

🕐

**Preparation: 15 minutes
Refrigeration:
20 minutes**

• Chop the **pistachios**. Mix the **honey** with the **orange flower water**.

• Peel the **clementines** with a very sharp knife and cut into slices.

• Mix all the ingredients together in a salad bowl. Let stand for 20 minutes in the refrigerator. Add the chopped **tarragon** and serve.

BLUEBERRY GRATIN

182 kcal/person

—

Vegetarian

—

Gluten free

Eggs
x 2

Milk
about 7 tablespoons
(100 mL)

Honey
1 tablespoon (20 g)

Almond flour
About ½ cup (50 g)

Blueberries
10½ ounces (300 g)

Preparation: 10 minutes
Cooking: 20 minutes

• Preheat the oven to 350°F/180°C.

• Beat together the **eggs**, **milk**, **honey**, and **almond flour**.

• Place the **blueberries** in the bottom of 4 small gratin dishes. Pour the egg mixture over and bake for 20 minutes. Serve warm or cold.

APRICOT AND ROSEMARY ROLLS

118 kcal/person

—

Vegetarian

—

Lactose free

Apricots
x 8

Brik pastry
4 sheets

Olive oil
¼ cup (60 mL)

Rosemary
4 small sprigs

Honey
2 tablespoons (40 g)

Preparation: 15 minutes
Cooking: 25 minutes

• Preheat the oven to 350°F/180°C. Pit the **apricots** and cut into pieces.

• Spread out the sheets of **brik pastry** and brush with **olive oil**. Arrange the **apricots** and chopped **rosemary** in the middle of each one. Cover with **honey**. Turn in the sides and roll up the pastry sheets tightly.

• Bake for 25 minutes. Serve hot.

MIXED FRUIT SALAD WITH CHAMPAGNE

161 kcal/person

—

Vegan

—

No added sugar

Watermelon
14 ounces (400 g)

Strawberries
14 ounces (400 g)

Blueberries
3½ ounces (100 g)

Pink grapefruit
x 1

Pink Champagne
17 fluid ounces (500 mL),
well chilled

Preparation: 10 minutes

• Seed and cut the **watermelon** into small pieces. Place in bowls with the hulled **strawberries**, cut into quarters, and the **blueberries**. Add the strained juice of the **grapefruit**.

• Refrigerate until ready to serve. Pour the **pink Champagne** into the bowls and serve immediately.

CHERRY CLAFOUTIS

133 kcal/person

—

Gluten free

Eggs
x 2

Milk
About 7 tablespoons
(100 mL)

Honey
1 tablespoon (20 g)

Almond flour
About ½ cup (50 g)

Cherries
x 60

Preparation: 20 minutes
Cooking: 25 minutes

• Preheat the oven to 350°F/180°C.

• Beat the **eggs**, **milk**, **honey**, and **almond flour**.

• Pit the **cherries** and place them in a gratin dish. Cover with the **egg** mixture and bake for 25 minutes. Serve warm or cold.

COCONUT AND CHOCOLATE BALLS

313 kcal/person

—

Vegetarian

—

Gluten free

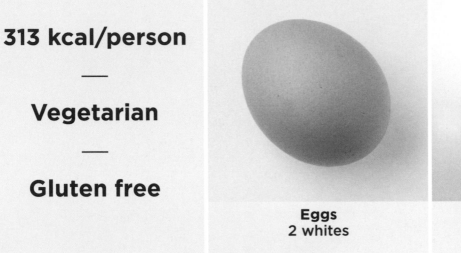

Eggs
2 whites

Honey
2 tablespoons (40 g)

Grated coconut
6 ounces (180 g)

Chocolate 70% cocoa
6 squares

Preparation: 15 minutes
Cooking: 5 minutes

• Preheat the oven to 410°F/210°C.
• Using your fingertips, mix the **egg whites** with the **honey** and **coconut**. Form into 12 balls and arrange on a baking sheet lined with parchment paper, leaving plenty of space in between.
• Insert one-half square of **chocolate** in the middle of each ball. Bake for 5 minutes. Cool before serving.

CHERRY SOUP WITH A MINT INFUSION

133 kcal/person

—

Gluten free

—

Lactose free

Red wine
2 cups (480 mL)

Honey
3 tablespoons (60 g)

Star anise
x 5

Mint
1 bunch

Cherries
x 32

Preparation: 15 minutes
Cooking: 25 minutes
Refrigeration: 1 hour

• Heat the **red wine**, **honey**, and **star anise** for 25 minutes over very low heat. Remove from the heat and add the whole bunch of **mint**, reserving a few sprigs for garnish. Infuse for 1 hour in the refrigerator. Remove the **mint**.

• Pit the **cherries**. Stir them into the wine mixture and serve garnished with the reserved **mint** sprigs.

APRICOTS WITH VANILLA AND LEMON

106 kcal/person

—

Vegan

Sweet white wine
2 cups (480 mL)

Vanilla
2 beans

Organic lemon
x 1

Apricots
x 8

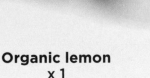

Preparation: 10 minutes
Cooking: 45 minutes
Refrigeration: 1 hour

• Pour the **white wine** into a saucepan. Add the **vanilla** (beans split open and scraped) and the zest and juice of the **lemon**. Bring to a boil and reduce by half over low heat.

• Pit the **apricots** and add them to the pan. Remove from the heat and let cool. Infuse in the refrigerator for 1 hour. Serve cold.

LYCHEES AND RASPBERRIES WITH CHAMPAGNE

110 kcal/person

—

Vegan

—

Gluten free

Lychees
x 20

Raspberries
9 ounces (250 g)

Mint
8 leaves

Pink Champagne
2 cups (480 mL), well chilled

Preparation: 15 minutes

• Peel the **lychees** and cut into pieces. Halve the **raspberries**. Slice the **mint** leaves and mix with the fruit. Divide into bowls.

• Refrigerate. Immediately before serving, pour the **pink Champagne** over the fruit.

BAKED APPLES

146 kcal/person

—

Lactose free

Cooking apples
x 4

Prunes
x 8 (pitted)

Slivered almonds
2 tablespoons (14 g)

Hazelnuts
x 20

Honey
¼ cup (80 g)

Preparation: 10 minutes
Cooking: 20 minutes

• Preheat the oven to 350°F/180°C.
• Cut "lids" off the **apples** and scoop out the flesh. Mix the flesh with the **prunes**, cut into small pieces, the **almonds**, chopped **hazelnuts**, and the **honey**.
• Stuff the **apples** with the mixture and bake for 20 minutes. Serve warm.

CHOCOLATE AND RASPBERRY MOUSSE

450 kcal/person

—

Gluten free

Eggs
x 6

Chocolate 70% cocoa
7 ounces (200 g)

Raspberries
7 ounces (200 g)

Preparation: 20 minutes
Refrigeration: 2 hours

• Separate the **eggs**. Melt the **chocolate** in a double boiler and mix with the yolks.
• Beat the **egg whites** until stiff and fold gently into the melted **chocolate**. Add the **raspberries**, cut into pieces.
• Divide the mousse among 4 ramekins and refrigerate for 2 hours.

APRICOTS WITH ALMONDS

64 kcal/person

—

Gluten free

—

Lactose free

Apricots
x 4

Honey
2 tablespoons (40 g)

Almond flour
3 tablespoons (18 g)

Slivered almonds
2 tablespoons (14 grams)

Preparation: 15 minutes
Cooking: 11 minutes

• Preheat the oven to 350°F/180°C. Halve the **apricots** and remove the pits.

• Heat the **honey** with the **almond flour** and **slivered almonds** for 1 minute over low heat, stirring with a spatula.

• Top the **apricot** halves with the **honey** and **almond** mixture and bake for 10 minutes. Serve warm or cold.

PASSION FRUIT WITH CHOCOLATE

105 kcal/person

Passion fruit
x 6

Chocolate 70% cocoa
4 squares

Low-fat cream
¼ cup (60 mL)

Preparation: 10 minutes
Cooking: 5 minutes
Refrigeration: 1 hour

• Halve the **passion fruit** and scoop out and reserve the pulp. Place the **chocolate** and **cream** in a heatproof bowl. Rest over a saucepan of simmering water to melt the **chocolate**, stirring with a spatula. Remove from the heat, add the reserved pulp, mix, and fill the **passion fruit** with this mixture. Refrigerate for 1 hour and serve.

LEMON SEMIFREDDO WITH RASPBERRIES

130 kcal/person

—

Gluten free

Lemons
x 4

Low-fat cream cheese
8½ ounces (240 g)

Raspberries
3½ ounces (100 g)

Honey
2 tablespoons (40 g)

Preparation: 15 minutes
Freezing: 1 hour,
15 minutes

• Cut "lids" off the **lemons**. Scoop out the contents with a very sharp knife and reserve the juice.
• Beat the **cream cheese** with the crushed **raspberries**, **honey**, and half the reserved **lemon** juice. Spoon into the **lemons** and freeze for 1 hour, 15 minutes. Serve semi-frozen, topped with "lids."

PEAR AND BLACKBERRY MILLEFEUILLES

91 kcal/person
—
No added sugar

Brik pastry
2 sheets

Vanilla
1 bean

Pears
x 2

Blackberries
3½ ounces (100 g)

Low-fat cream cheese
4¼ ounces (120 g)

1 tablespoon olive oil

Preparation: 10 minutes
Cooking: 5 minutes

• Preheat the oven to 400°F/200°C. Brush the **brik pastry** sheets with olive oil. Bake for 5 minutes until golden and break into 12 pieces.
• Split the **vanilla bean** lengthwise and scrape the seeds.
• Mix the **pears**, cut into pieces, with the crushed **blackberries**, the **cream cheese**, and the **vanilla** seeds. Arrange spoonfuls of the fruit mixture on plates with pieces of **pastry** in between.

FRUIT SALAD WITH ROSÉ WINE

222 kcal/person

—

Vegan

—

No added sugar

Cantaloupe melons
x 2

Blueberries
3½ ounces (100 g)

Raspberries
7 ounces (200 g)

Watermelon
7 ounces (200 g)

Rosé wine
2 cups (480 mL)

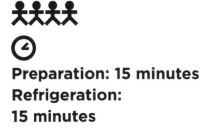

Preparation: 15 minutes
Refrigeration:
15 minutes

• Halve the **cantaloupe melons**. Scoop out the seeds, remove the flesh, and, cut into small pieces. Mix the cantaloupe with the **blueberries**, the halved **raspberries**, and the seeded and chopped **watermelon**.
• Spoon the fruit into the **melon** halves. Pour the **rosé wine** over and refrigerate for 15 minutes before serving.

NECTARINE GRATIN WITH PINE NUTS

116 kcal/person

—

Gluten free

—

Lactose free

Honey
2 tablespoons (40 g)

Orange flower water
3 tablespoons (45 mL)

Nectarines
x 4

Almond flour
3 tablespoons (18 g)

Pine nuts
3 tablespoons (27 g)

Preparation: 15 minutes
Cooking: 21 minutes

• Preheat the oven to 350°F/180°C. Heat the **honey** and the **orange flower water** in a saucepan over low heat for 1 minute.

• Pit the **nectarines** and cut into segments. Arrange in an ovenproof dish. Sprinkle with **almond flour** and **pine nuts**. Pour the **honey** and **orange flower water** mixture over and bake for 20 minutes. Serve warm.

ICED DESSERT WITH MIXED BERRIES

116 kcal/person

—

Gluten free

Mixed berries
9 ounces (250 g)

Low-fat cream cheese
4¼ ounces (120 g)

Egg
2 whites

Honey
2 tablespoons plus
1 teaspoon (50 g)

Preparation: 25 minutes
Freezing: Overnight

• Mix the crushed **berries** with the **cream cheese**. Beat the **egg whites** until stiff, then add the warmed **honey**, while beating for 1 minute more.
• Fold the egg white mixture into the **cream cheese** and **berry** mixture. Transfer to a mold and freeze overnight. Serve in thick slices.

354

BAKED CHOCOLATE MOUSSE

450 kcal/person

Eggs
x 6

Chocolate 70% cocoa
7 ounces (200 g)

Cocoa powder (unsweetened)
2 tablespoons (10 g)

Preparation: 15 minutes
Cooking: 9 minutes

• Preheat the oven to 400°F/200°C. Separate the **eggs**. Melt the **chocolate** in a double boiler and mix it with the **egg** yolks.

• Beat the whites until stiff and fold gently into the melted **chocolate**.

• Transfer the mousse to ramekins and bake for 9 minutes. Sprinkle with **cocoa powder** and serve warm.

PEAR GRANITA

65 kcal/person

—

Vegan

—

No added sugar

Pears
x 4 (very ripe)

Lemon
x 1

Basil
8 leaves

Preparation: 15 minutes

• Peel the **pears** and cut into pieces. Mix pieces with the juice of the **lemon**. Refrigerate.

• Just before serving, put half the **pear** pieces in bowls. Purée the remaining **pear** in a blender with the **basil** and 15 ice cubes.

• Top the **pear** pieces with the granita and serve immediately.

INDEX

A

Black Dog & Leventhal Publishers
Hachette Book Group
1290 Avenue of the Americas
New York, NY 10104

www.hachettebookgroup.com
www.blackdogandleventhal.com

First published in France in 2016 by Hachette Livre (Hachette Pratique)
First U.S. Edition: November 2017

Black Dog & Leventhal Publishers is an imprint of Hachette Books, a division of Hachette Book Group. The Black Dog & Leventhal Publishers name and logo are trademarks of Hachette Book Group, Inc.

The publisher is not responsible for websites (or their content) that are not owned by the publisher.

The Hachette Speakers Bureau provides a wide range of authors for speaking events. To find out more, go to www.HachetteSpeakersBureau.com or call (866) 376-6591.

Print book interior design by Marie-Paule Jaulme

Library of Congress Control Number: 2017939984

ISBN: 978-0-316-51025-7 (hardcover)

Printed in China

IM

10 9 8 7 6 5 4 3 2 1